> There is properly no history,
> only biography.
> — *Ralph Waldo Emerson*

* * * * * * * * * * * * * * * * *

he Making of America series traces the constitutional history of the United States through overlapping biographies of American men and women. The debates that raged when our nation was founded have been argued ever since: *How should the Constitution be interpreted? What is the meaning, and where are the limits, of personal liberty? What is the proper role of the federal government? Who should be included in "we the people"?* Each biography in the series tells the story of an American leader who helped shape the United States of today.

Abraham Lincoln, lithograph by J. H. Bufford's Sons, 1865

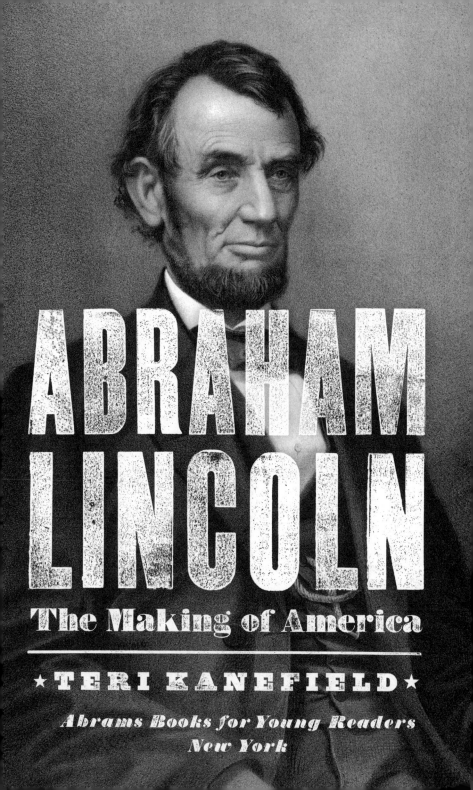

ABRAHAM LINCOLN

The Making of America

★ TERI KANEFIELD ★

Abrams Books for Young Readers
New York

For Andy

✳ ✳ ✳ ✳ ✳ ✳ ✳ ✳ ✳

All images used in this book are public domain.

Cataloging-in-Publication Data has been applied for
and may be obtained from the Library of Congress.

ISBN 978-1-4197-3159-4

Text copyright © 2018 Teri Kanefield

Book design by Sara Corbett

Printed and bound in USA
10 9 8 7 6 5 4 3 2 1

Abrams Books for Young Readers are available at special discounts when
purchased in quantity for premiums and promotions as well as fundraising
or educational use. Special editions can also be created to specification.
For details, contact specialsales@abramsbooks.com or the address below.

Abrams® and The Making of America® are registered trademarks of Harry N. Abrams, Inc.

ABRAMS The Art of Books
195 Broadway, New York, NY 10007
abramsbooks.com

CONTENTS

Lithograph, by J.H. Buffond Sons, 1865 (Library of Congress)

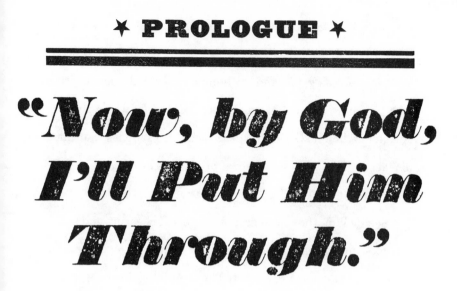

"Now, by God, I'll Put Him Through."

On April 11, 1865, a crowd gathered in front of the White House, calling for President Abraham Lincoln to give a speech. For two days the nation had been rocked by the news that Confederate general Robert E. Lee had surrendered to Union general Ulysses S. Grant. Everyone understood this meant that the Civil War was at last ending. The day before, Lincoln dodged requests for a speech, but this evening he heeded the call and stepped to the window. At his side was his twelve-year-old son, Tad.

Lincoln was gaunt and rawboned, described once as "thin as a beanpole and ugly as a scarecrow," but he was a riveting speaker. When he began to speak, the deep sadness that lined his face and the sorrowful aspect of his eyes lifted, and his face came alive.

Seeing him, the crowd erupted with joy, cheering and swaying, glowing with adoration, waiting for the stirring and poetic words they had come to expect. The crowd was diverse—blacks and whites together cheering the president who, two years earlier, signed the Emancipation Proclamation and was now throwing his weight and influence behind a new amendment to the Constitution that would forever abolish slavery in the United States.

Not everyone in the crowd, however, was feeling joyous. Standing among the cheering throngs was a man named John Wilkes Booth. Booth, a well-known actor, had spent some of his youth in the South. He was a passionate supporter of the Confederacy and a strong believer that blacks belonged in slavery. Like former vice president John Calhoun, he believed that slavery was a "positive good."

For Booth, elevating the status of blacks was an insult to white people and a step in the direction of destroying the white race. "This country," Booth said once, "was formed for the white, not for the black man." He also wrote, "Our cause being almost lost, something decisive and great must be done." He hated Lincoln with a passion.

"We meet this evening," Lincoln began, "not in sorrow, but in gladness of heart." Then, instead of launching into the stirring victory speech many in the crowd expected, he spoke somberly on the difficult topic of how to bring the Southern states back into the Union.

Lincoln didn't come right out and say that blacks should be given the right to vote. Instead he dropped hints, saying, "It is also unsatisfactory to some that the elective franchise is not given to the colored man." He talked about the proposed amendment to the Constitution that would ban slavery, and concluded by saying, "In the present situation, as the phrase goes, it may be my duty to make some new announcement to the people of the South. I am considering, and shall not fail to act, when satisfied that action will be proper."

Booth caught Lincoln's drift. He turned to his companion, a former Confederate soldier named Lewis Powell, and said, "That means n— citizenship. Now, by God, I'll put him through. That is the last speech he will ever make."

✳ ✳ ✳ ✳ ✳ ✳ ✳ ✳ ✳ ✳ ✳ ✳ ✳ ✳ ✳

Four days later on the evening of April 14, 1865, Lincoln made plans to attend a play called *Our American Cousin* at Ford's Theatre in Washington. John Wilkes Booth had plans of his own. Learning that Lincoln would be at the theater, he, too, intended to be there—with a fully loaded .44 caliber pistol.

A Boy on the Frontier

When first my father settled here,
'Twas then the frontier line:
The panther's scream filled night with fear
And bears preyed on the swine.

— Abraham Lincoln

he man who John Wilkes Booth planned to kill was born on February 12, 1809, in a one-room log cabin on a small, isolated farm deep in the backwoods of Kentucky. The cabin had a dirt floor and one window without glass. The land was rocky and poor—"a barren waste . . . save some little patches on the creek bottoms." Abraham—who disliked the nickname Abe—lived with his parents and his sister, Sarah, who was two years older. He would have had a younger brother as well, but Thomas died while still a baby.

Abraham's parents had trouble growing enough food to feed the family, so when he was still a toddler, the Lincolns moved ten miles north in search of more fertile land. They settled on the banks of Knob Creek, a stream so clear you could see a pebble at the bottom ten feet down. While stunningly beautiful, the land wasn't much better for farming, with deep hollows and ravines, surrounded by gorges that often flooded.

Neighbors described the Lincolns as among "the very poorest people." Abraham later recalled when "my toes stuck out through my broken shoes in winter; when my arms were out at the elbows; when I shivered with the cold." The Lincolns lived near the Cumberland Trail, the road leading from Nashville, Tennessee to Louisville, Kentucky.

Lincoln Cabin, Birth Place of Abraham Lincoln, from a postcard published by the Kraemer Art Company, Cincinnati, Ohio, date unknown

Abraham saw slave traders driving coffles of enslaved men and women along the trail.

Abraham's family belonged to the Separate Baptist Church. They believed in predestination and followed a strict code of behavior condemning profanity, drunkenness, gossip, and horse racing. Not long before Abraham was born, there was a split in the local Baptist church over slavery. The Lincolns went with the antislavery group. Abraham absorbed his church's strict standards of behavior and antislavery sentiments. "I am naturally anti-slavery," he later remarked. "If slavery is not wrong, nothing is wrong. I cannot remember when I did not so think and feel."

✷ ✷ ✷ ✷ ✷ ✷ ✷ ✷ ✷ ✷ ✷ ✷ ✷ ✷ ✷

Abraham's roots went deep in American history. The first Lincolns came from Norwich, England in 1637 and settled in Massachusetts. Some of Abraham's ancestors were Pennsylvania Quakers. His paternal grandparents settled in Virginia before moving to Kentucky to seek their fortunes. These grandparents headed west after a distant relative, Daniel Boone, told them about wide expanses of land on the other side of the Appalachian Mountains. When settlers from Virginia poured into what is now Kentucky and wrested the land from the Shawnee and other tribes, Abraham's paternal grandfather joined a militia and fought the native people.

The family legend that, in Abraham's words, was "more strongly than all the others imprinted upon my mind and memory," was the story of how his paternal grandfather died in

Daniel Boone Escorting Settlers Through the Cumberland Gap, by George Caleb Bingham, 1851–1852. The trail took settlers through the Appalachian Mountains from Virginia to Kentucky.

an Indian attack. The story went like this: Abraham's grand-father was planting a cornfield not far from a Kentucky fort called Hughes Station with his three sons, Josiah, Mordecai, and Thomas, when an Indian shot him from the woods. The Indian who killed him was a Shawnee—a member of the tribe that had been driven from the land that Lincoln farmed. After the shot was fired, fourteen-year-old Mordecai ran to a nearby cabin and peeked from between the logs. He saw his youngest brother, six-year-old Thomas, sobbing over their dead father's body—and an Indian coming from the woods toward the child. Mordecai grabbed a flintlock rifle, poked the muzzle between the logs, aimed at a silver pendant the Indian wore on his chest, and fired. He killed the Indian. The child, Thomas Lincoln, would become father to America's sixteenth president.

Thomas grew into a "plain unpretending plodding man." He spent years working as a day laborer until he saved enough to buy his own farm. He never learned to read or write. The first woman he proposed to, Sarah Bush, could read and was consid-ered well educated by the standards of the community. After she turned him down, he proposed to Nancy Hanks, who accepted him. Nancy, a quiet and sad woman, was described by neighbors as "a woman known for the extraordinary strength of her mind among the family and all who knew her; she was superior to her husband in every way."

★   ★   ★   ★   ★   ★   ★   ★   ★   ★   ★   ★   ★   ★   ★

braham was seven years old when the Lincolns were driven out of Kentucky by a lawsuit: Wealthier settlers claimed to be the rightful owners of the Lincoln farm. Thomas Lincoln didn't have the money to pay a lawyer to prove that he had bought the land. The problem, as Thomas understood it, was slaveholders who wanted to enlarge their plantations by pushing away their poor neighbors who owned no slaves and worked the fields themselves. Lawyers wanted to work for the plantation owners, who had plenty of money for legal fees. Thomas Lincoln didn't want to fight with large plantation owners, and—having no wish to be a slave owner himself—he had no desire to try to join their ranks. The only solution was to leave Kentucky.

The Lincolns were thus in desperate need of a new home when President James Madison, the fourth president of the United States, announced that lands in the Indiana Territory would be offered to settlers. The settlers would be able to buy their land directly from the federal government, so they would have proof of their purchase and recorded title to their property, which meant they wouldn't have to worry about any more ejection lawsuits.

Thomas Lincoln journeyed northward across the Ohio River to stake his claim. Indiana was still mostly pathless and unbroken. Thomas selected a site in the little community of Pigeon Creek in southern Indiana, a land dense with maple, hickory, and oak trees. As was customary, he burned trees to mark the boundaries of his claim and piled brush on the corners of his new tract.

After he arrived back home, the family packed their household possessions into a wagon: A feather bed, a spinning wheel, a skillet, a Dutch oven, a kettle, dishes, and other small household items. They left on a cold day in December with their wagon, cow, and four horses. When they reached the Ohio River at what is now Cloverport, Kentucky, they crossed on a makeshift ferry. Once in Indiana, they passed through forests so thick with tangled underbrush that they had to hack a trail with axes.

Upon arriving at their tract of land, they built a crude lean-to cabin. Because of the freezing weather, they could not properly seal the spaces between the logs with clay and grass, so all winter bitter winds swept through. The family survived by hunting deer and bears.

Other relatives, including Nancy's maternal aunt and uncle,

also lost their homes through ejection lawsuits, so they, too, staked claims in Indiana and moved north. When spring came, the settlers helped each other build sturdier log cabins. Next they faced the daunting task of clearing away trees and undergrowth so they could plant corn.

Abraham was expected to do his share. He was eight, but large and strong for his age. An axe was put in his hand and he fought "the trees and logs and grubs . . . until he reached his twentieth year."

★ ★ ★ ★ ★ ★ ★ ★ ★ ★ ★ ★ ★ ★ ★

Tragedy struck when Nancy Lincoln fell ill with what was then known as milk sickness—she became dizzy with stomach pains, trembling, and irregular breathing. The settlers understood that the illness was somehow connected to milk, but they didn't understand that cows eating the poisonous white snakeroot plant caused the problem. Nancy held on for about two weeks. When she knew she was on the brink of death, she called Abraham and Sarah to her. She told them to be kind to their father, to one another, and to the world. She died on October 5, 1818. Abraham was nine years old.

A devastated Abraham took to reciting his mother's favorite

Bible stories, for they brought back memories of her voice. His sister Sarah tried to keep house, but she often sat by the fire, crying. A cousin, Dennis Hanks, moved in to help with the chores, but the Lincoln household fell into disarray.

Life improved the following year when Thomas Lincoln returned to Kentucky to propose marriage to the woman who had once rejected him, Sarah Bush Johnston—who was now a widow with three children. His proposal, delivered while she was doing laundry, was straight to the point and unsentimental. "I have no wife," he told her, "and you have no husband. I came a purpose to marry you. I knowed you from a gal and you knowed me from a boy—I have no time to lose and if you are willing, let it be done straight off." This time she accepted him and they were married on December 2, 1819.

After the ceremony, they journeyed together to Indiana, bringing Sarah's three children: twelve-year-old Elizabeth, nine-year-old John, and seven-year-old Matilda. Upon their arrival, Sarah found Abraham and his sister "wild and ragged," and in need of a good washing. "The first time I saw Abe," she said, "he was the ugliest chap that ever obstructed my view." She took a special liking to Abraham, saying he was the most well-behaved boy she had ever seen.

A school opened about a mile from the Lincolns' house, and all the youngsters in the household attended sporadically. "I never went to school more than six months in my life," Abraham said later, "but I can say this: that among my earliest recollections, I remember how, when a mere child, I used to get irritated when anybody talked to me in a way I could not understand."

Abraham, who was mostly self-taught, developed a passion for books and reading. His love of reading put him at odds with his father and stepbrother. Both Thomas Lincoln and John Johnston believed "bone and muscle sufficient to make the man" and that "time spent in school was double wasted." Johnston could not understand how Abraham could care about "some old musty books," and he was convinced that Abraham's love of reading was "clear proof of Abe's insanity." Thomas Lincoln saw his son's reading as a waste of time, coming from a lazy desire to sit and do nothing instead of working. "I ain't got no education," Thomas Lincoln said, "but I get along far better than if I had." He added that "if Abe don't fool away all his time on books, he may make something yet." He sometimes whipped Abraham for what he called laziness.

But young Abraham had a stubborn streak. When his father tried to break his habit of reading, he dug in his heels and resisted. Ignoring the ridicule of his father and stepbrother, he read every book he could get his hands on, starting with the few his stepmother brought from Kentucky, and then borrowing books from neighbors. He read *Pilgrim's Progress*, a volume of *Aesop's Fables*, *The Arabian Nights*, and *Robinson Crusoe*. Because he had so few books, he reread the ones he had until he had memorized entire passages.

Abraham rejected the popular backwoods pastimes. He disliked hunting and cared nothing for guns. He exhibited other qualities considered odd in a backwoods boy. He was unusually sensitive, reacting strongly to cruelty to animals. When his stepbrother crushed a turtle for sport, Abraham "quivered all over" and explained that even an "ant's life was to it as sweet as ours to us."

Abraham, quiet and introspective, withdrew into himself for long periods. He fell in love with poetry. He read and memorized poems and wrote his own rhymes. As a teenager, he wrote:

Abraham Lincoln
His hand and pen
He will be good but
God knows when.

And:

> *Abraham Lincoln is my name*
> *And with my pen I wrote the same*
> *I wrote it in both haste and speed*
> *And left it here for fools to read.*

While Thomas Lincoln bonded with his stepson, finding that he had more in common with Johnston than his own son, Abraham and his stepmother formed a bond of their own. Sarah often protected Abraham from his father's anger. Abraham described his stepmother as his best friend in the world, and said that no son could love a mother more than he loved her.

★ ★ ★ ★ ★ ★ ★ ★ ★ ★ ★ ★ ★ ★

Abraham grew so large and strong that he could beat the other boys in races, wrestling, and other sports. He could "sink an axe deeper into a tree and strike a heavier blow with a maul than anyone." His physical strength and intelligence made him a natural leader. In the words of one contemporary, he "soared above us. He naturally assumed the leadership of the boys."

None of this helped him with the girls, though, who found him unattractive and awkward. Whenever he tried to "go with" a girl, she'd "give him the mitten every time." Abraham remained good humored. When the girls made fun of his looks, he laughed with them and made jokes at his own expense—which he continued to do throughout his life. Years later, when a political opponent called him two-faced, he said, "I leave it to my audience. If I had two faces, would I wear this one?" Another time he joked that the Lord preferred common-looking people, which was why he made so many more of them.

A Strange and Penniless Boy

*It would astonish if not amuse the older citizens to learn
that I (a strange, friendless, uneducated, penniless boy,
working at ten dollars per month) have been put down as the
candidate of pride, wealth, and aristocratic family distinction.*

— Abraham Lincoln

hen Abraham was fifteen, his father lent money to a friend who was unable to repay the loan, sending the Lincolns' finances into a downward spiral. To get out of trouble, Thomas put Abraham to work as a hired hand. For the next few years, a miserable Abraham worked as a butcher, woodchopper, and farmhand. By law, he had to turn his wages over to his father. He became angry and bitter over what he called "parental tyranny." He came to hate the heavy labor and drudgery of farmwork.

A Strange and Penniless Boy

He comforted himself with books. After working hard all day, he often read until past midnight. By this time, he was reading political biographies and histories. He read William Grimshaw's *History of the United States*, a biography of politician Henry Clay, and Parson Weem's biography of George Washington. He wrote an essay—now lost—on national politics.

The Boyhood of Lincoln—
An Evening in the Log Hut,
by Eastman Johnson, 1868

He also found time to build a small boat with a friend. The boat caught the attention of two gentlemen traveling through town, who asked Abraham to row them and their trunks to a steamer on the Ohio River. Abraham readily agreed. After he rowed the men to their steamer, they stunned him by tossing two silver half dollars into his boat—an unheard of sum of money for a few hours' work. "It was the most important incident in my life," Abraham said later. "I could scarcely credit that I, a poor boy, had earned a dollar in less than a day."

He took to rowing other passengers to their steamers—until one day he was arrested and brought to court for operating a ferry without a license. The judge pulled a statute book from the shelf and found a loophole in the law: It was illegal for unlicensed persons from operating ferries from one riverbank to the other, but the law said nothing about rowing passengers partway across the river. The judge was thus able to find Abraham not guilty. All of this stimulated Abraham's curiosity about the law. He borrowed a copy of the Statutes of Indiana and read the entire volume.

★   ★   ★   ★   ★   ★   ★   ★   ★   ★   ★   ★   ★   ★   ★

 braham was nineteen when his world was again rocked with grief. His sister, Sarah, who eighteen months earlier had married a young man named Aaron Grigsby, died in childbirth. When Abraham learned of her death, he "sat down on a log and hid his face in his hands while the tears rolled down through his long bony fingers. Those present turned away in pity and left him to his grief." He suffered a lengthy bout of what was then called melancholy, but today is called depression. Reserved and inward by nature, he said very little about the deaths of either his mother or his sister. Later though, he wrote, "In this sad world of ours, sorrow comes to all; and to the young, it comes with bitterest agony because it takes them unawares. I have had experience enough to know what I say."

He dealt with his grief by plunging into his work. His job at the time was clerking in a store owned by a prosperous merchant. As a shopkeeper, he had access to newspapers, which he devoured. Stores in frontier towns were often social gathering places where men met to discuss the pressing questions of the day: Should women be educated? Was slavery right or wrong? Should the federal government raise money for building roads and canals?

The year Sarah died in childbirth, 1828, was the year General Andrew Jackson won the presidency against the incumbent president John Quincy Adams. Jackson, the hero of the Battle of New Orleans, championed the rights of farmers and frontiersmen.

Jackson's political opponents, John Quincy Adams and Henry Clay, in contrast, represented the interests of cities and industry, advocating what Henry Clay called "the American System"—a plan for strengthening industry and commerce through a strong national bank and federally funded internal improvements like roads and canals.

Thomas Lincoln—and indeed most of the Lincolns' friends and neighbors—were Jackson supporters. On the other hand, William Jones, the prosperous merchant who owned the store where Abraham worked, passionately supported Henry Clay. Abraham and Jones had long, thoughtful political discussions. Soon Abraham, too, was an admirer of Clay and the American System. One historian concluded that Abraham rejected Jackson's ideals because he associated them with rural backwardness, lack of education, and his father's way of life, while he associated Henry Clay's American System with ambitious and enterprising merchants and lawyers.

Abraham thus turned his back on the political ideals of his father and neighbors, but all his life he carried a deep understanding of the rural Democrats. His understanding of the fears and hopes of Andrew Jackson's admirers later served him well.

★ ★ ★ ★ ★ ★ ★ ★ ★ ★ ★ ★ ★ ★

L ate in 1828, a wealthy merchant named James Gentry needed someone to help his son take a cargo boat to New Orleans. He offered the job to Abraham. Abraham accepted and spent two weeks building a flatboat with Gentry's son, Allen. Then in December of 1828, Allen and Abraham set off down the river. On their way to New Orleans, they fought off a band of would-be robbers.

Abraham's first time in a large city opened his eyes to the world beyond his backwoods farm and community. He was awed by the row of ships and bustling waterfront, but disgusted by the sight of a slave auction. He was silent for a while, taking in the sight of the auction. Then he turned to Allen and said, "That is a disgrace."

A Slave Father Sold Away from His Family, artist unknown, 1860

A Strange and Penniless Boy

* * * * * * * * * * * * * * *

Relatives of Abraham's mother, the Hanks family, moved to Decatur, Illinois, and sent back letters with glowing descriptions of lush, fertile soil. In 1830, when a new bout of milk sickness broke out in southern Indiana, Thomas Lincoln decided to move his family once more, this time to Illinois. In early spring, he sold his Indiana land and farm, and the Lincolns piled their possessions into a wagon. Abraham, now an adult and no longer legally bound to work for his father, could have struck out on his own, but his father was growing feeble and losing his sight and desperately needed Abraham's help. Abraham remained with his family out of duty to his father and affection for his stepmother.

Friends and neighbors came to see them off. The journey to Illinois took them over swollen and still-frozen rivers and rugged terrain. Two weeks and more than two hundred exhausting miles later, they arrived in Decatur, a town consisting of fewer than a dozen log cabins. Most of the population was scattered in the outlying areas. The Lincolns' new land was about ten miles from town. Abraham spent the summer helping his father and cousins break up about ten acres for planting. He then split rails to fence it in—grueling, backbreaking work.

Lincoln the Rail Splitter, by J. L. G. Ferris, 1909

Abraham found time to make friends among their new neighbors. That summer he also made his political debut. One day, two candidates for the state legislature offered speeches in front of a small crowd. One of the candidates, John F. Posey, annoyed the audience when he failed to offer alcoholic refreshments. Abraham's new friends urged him to take the stage. They expected him to use his wit and humor to ridicule Posey. Lincoln said he would make a speech as long as his friends wouldn't laugh at him. When they agreed, he took the stage. Wearing tow-linen pants, a hickory shirt, and a straw hat, he made the best speech of the day. Instead of ridiculing Posey, he spoke well of both candidates and urged the citizens—in the spirit of Henry Clay's American System—to improve the Sangamon River for transportation. While no record of the exact words of Lincoln's first political speech exists, his listeners were surprised and entertained by his warmth and humor.

In August, Decatur was attacked by a swarm of gallinippers—the frontier word for malaria-carrying mosquitoes. Abraham's father and stepmother fell ill, suffering terribly with the disease the locals called the Illinois shakes. After they recovered, a December blizzard dumped three feet of snow on the Lincoln farm followed by freezing rain and a long bitter winter.

That was it for Thomas Lincoln. He had enough of Illinois.
The winters were too cold and the mosquitoes too brutal. When
spring came, he made plans to move his family back to Indiana.
Abraham—now twenty-two years old—did not return with them.
He and his stepbrother, Johnston, decided to remain in Illinois.
Abraham's stepmother tied his earthly possessions into a bundle.
Abraham ran a stick through the knot, threw it over his shoulder,
and said goodbye to his father and stepmother.

Entering Politics

*I have no other [ambition] so great
as that of being truly esteemed of
my fellow men, by rendering myself
worthy of their esteem.*

— Abraham Lincoln

braham Lincoln entered New Salem, the village that
would become his home for the next six years, with a
splash—literally. He, Johnston, and one of their Hanks
cousins had taken a job transporting a flatboat of cargo
down the Sangamon River. They were floating down the
river loaded with barrels of bacon, wheat, and corn when the boat
got stuck in a milldam and took on water. The three young men
worked frantically to save the cargo. Lincoln, wearing a big pair

New Salem, Home of Abraham Lincoln 1831, by Arthur L. Brown, 1909

of cowhide boots, took charge of the rescue operation. First they transferred the cargo to a borrowed boat, and then drained the water. Without the water and cargo, the boat lifted high enough to glide over the milldam. The villagers who turned out to watch the spectacle cheered when the young men saved the cargo.

Denton Offutt, the man who had hired them for the adventure, was so impressed when he learned that Lincoln saved the cargo that he decided to open a store in New Salem and put Lincoln in charge. Lincoln accepted the job.

After delivering the cargo, Lincoln returned to New Salem, arriving in the summer of 1831. As was customary for single young men, he boarded with various families, doing household and farming chores in exchange for a bed. The village of New Salem consisted of about two dozen families, three stores, a saloon, and a blacksmith shop. About one hundred people lived in the town

NEW SALEM
HOME OF
ABRAHAM LINCOLN
1831 to 1837

itself, with the rest of the population scattered in the rural out-skirts. Lincoln was well liked and earned a reputation for telling jokes and entertaining stories.

While waiting for his new boss to send goods for the store, he took odd jobs. One potential employer asked if he could write. He replied, "I can make a few rabbit tracks," whereupon he was offered the job of clerk at the polls on Election Day. Ballots then were not secret. Voters stated their choice aloud. Most were ardent supporters of Andrew Jackson, who was then running for his second term as president. When it was time for Lincoln to vote, he announced himself for Jackson's opponent, Henry Clay.

When at last Offutt rented a log cabin and provided the goods for sale, Lincoln opened the store, stocking the shelves with coffee, tea, sugar, salt, seeds, tools, saddles, liquor, guns, gunpowder, and other general goods. He soon earned the nick-name that would stick for the remainder of his life: Honest Abe. One time he realized a woman overpaid for a dress, so he went in search of her and refunded her the difference. On another occa-sion, a woman asked for a pound of tea and Lincoln accidentally used the half-pound weight rather than the pound weight. When he realized his mistake, he went to her home and gave her another half pound of tea.

Lincoln's store became a favorite meeting place for local residents. Debating clubs were then springing up all over the nation. Lincoln participated in the local club and improved his speaking and debating skills. He was a slow and deliberate speaker, but learned to sprinkle his responses with humor and anecdotes. He still spoke with a Kentucky twang, which he retained his entire life.

Curious about the law, he often attended local court sessions. Once, after watching a renowned lawyer perform in the courtroom, Lincoln waited to shake the lawyer's hand. Later he said, "I felt that if I could ever make as good a speech as that, my soul would be satisfied." He believed his scanty education put the legal profession beyond his reach.

One day Lincoln's boss, Denton Offutt, bragged that Lincoln could outwrestle the town champion, Jack Armstrong. Lincoln agreed to the match, knowing it was something of a frontier rite of passage and a way for a newcomer in town to prove himself. Most of the town turned out to watch Lincoln and Armstrong wrestle. The combatants pushed and pulled and circled each other, getting each other into holds, until it became clear that Lincoln was the stronger of the two. Eventually Armstrong, in frustration, broke his hold. Under the loose rules of frontier wrestling, Lincoln could easily have become the winner. Instead he offered to shake hands with Armstrong and call the match a draw. No surprise—Lincoln's popularity increased.

Because New Salem was conveniently located on a river, it had the potential to become an important center for trade. Lincoln worried, though, that the river would not remain passable for larger boats unless the river was cleared of debris and straightened where the waterway turned sharp corners. While residents in the outlying areas were mostly Jacksonian Democrats who distrusted government programs, the townspeople agreed with Lincoln that improving the river would benefit the region. A group of town residents asked him to run for the state legislature, called the Assembly. So at the age of twenty-three, Lincoln announced himself a candidate for the state Assembly with a notice in the *Sangamo Journal*. "No person will deny," he wrote, "that the poorest and most thinly populated counties would be greatly benefited by the opening of good roads, and in the clearing of navigable streams." The problem was how to pay for it. He speculated that the cost couldn't be much, and besides, would be well worth it.

Three months before the election, panic erupted among the townspeople when the word spread that members of the Meskwaki Nation had left their settlements in Iowa and were returning to reclaim their ancestral lands in Illinois. The native people

Battle of Bad Axe, by Ernest Heinemann, circa 1876. The Black Hawk War ended with the defeat of the native people at the Battle of Bad Axe on August 2, 1832.

understood that they had been tricked into giving up their lands in 1804, and now they wanted it back.

The governor of Illinois, John Reynolds, hearing that the Meskwaki people were returning to reclaim their lands, called for volunteer soldiers. Lincoln enlisted in what was later called the Black Hawk War. The other recruits elected him captain, thus earning him a military title. He served a total of two-and-a-half months, but he saw no combat. Later he quipped that he became a "military hero" after "charges upon the wild onions" and "a good many bloody struggles with the mosquitoes."

After the Meskwakis were driven from Illinois, Lincoln returned to New Salem. With weeks remaining before the election, he took to the campaign trail. He stuck to the rural districts where he felt more at ease. His speeches were generally simple and to the point, like this one:

I presume you all know who I am. I am humble Abraham Lincoln. I have been solicited by many friends to become a candidate for the legislature. My politics are short and sweet, like the old woman's dance. I am in favor of a

After President Thomas Jefferson acquired the Louisiana Territory in 1804, American settlers poured into the prairies of the Meskwaki and Sauk tribal lands. A battle between the settlers and the Indians resulted in tribal members killing three white settlers in the area that is now St. Louis, Missouri. The tribal chiefs—who did not approve of the killings—feared that the American army would launch a bloody retaliation, so they sent five men as representatives to make peace. The five representatives had the authority to offer apologies and compensation to the families of the victims.

The two sides later gave different versions of what

national bank. I am in favor of the internal improvement

system . . . If elected, I shall be thankful; if not it will be

all the same.

Lincoln's belief in federally funded government programs

put him in direct opposition to the majority of those in Illinois,

who, like President Andrew Jackson, distrusted government as a

hotbed of political corruption, and wanted as little government

as possible. The Democrats did not want a federal bank, and

they did not want federal money spent on internal improvements.

happened during the talks. U.S. officials claimed the

representatives of the tribes willingly signed a treaty ceding

fifty million acres of tribal lands. The Sauk and Meskwaki

claimed the representatives were tricked into signing a treaty

they didn't understand. Moreover, the Sauk and Meskwaki

pointed out, the representatives did not have authority to sign

such a treaty, which followed none of the procedures required

by the Sauk and Meskwaki Nation for it to be considered

valid. The United States, however, held the tribes to the

treaty, forcing the Sauk and Meskwaki Nation to abandon

their lands in Illinois and move into what is now Iowa.

Many Jacksonian Democrats believed that the only action the federal government should undertake was aggressive expansion of the U.S. borders.

★ ★ ★ ★ ★ ★ ★ ★ ★ ★ ★ ★ ★ ★ ★

Lincoln was disappointed but not surprised when the votes were counted and he lost, coming in eighth in a field of thirteen. The top four candidates became representatives. Many of his rivals had the endorsements of influential Illinois politicians. Lincoln had only his ever-widening circle of friends and admirers. Lincoln's solace was that he won his hometown of New Salem by a landslide, tallying two hundred seventy-seven out of three hundred votes. He understood he lost the election because he was unknown outside New Salem. Lincoln, who badly wanted to make his mark in politics, knew it was time to venture out of the safety of his home community and make himself more widely known.

The quarrel over whether the Constitution required a small and weak federal government or whether the federal government had the power to undertake internal improvements dated back to the founding of the nation. Thomas Jefferson believed that there was nothing in the Constitution giving the federal government power to create a bank or national building projects. His rival, Alexander Hamilton, believed that the "general welfare" phrase in the Constitution justified government projects, as long as they promoted the public good.

The Jacksonian Democrats' views on government put them squarely in the tradition of Thomas Jefferson, while Lincoln followed in the footsteps of Alexander Hamilton.

A Lawyer

*Let reverence for the laws be breathed by
every American mother to the lisping babe that
prattles on her lap—let it be taught in schools,
in seminaries, and in colleges; let it be written
in primers, spelling books, and in almanacs;
let it be preached from the pulpit, proclaimed
in legislative halls, and enforced
in courts of justice.*

— Abraham Lincoln

incoln's store did not last long. Offutt failed to keep

the store adequately stocked, and in less than a year,

he abandoned it altogether, leaving Lincoln, at the age

of twenty-three, without a job. Lincoln tried opening

another store with a business partner, but that venture,

in Lincoln's words "winked out" when his partner used the profits

to buy whiskey, and then died from too much drinking, leaving

Lincoln in debt. By law Lincoln was only required to pay half the

debt, but out of consideration for the people who had trusted him and his partner with their money, he insisted on paying it all, a heavy burden that took him years to work off.

He was back to working at odd jobs, splitting rails, picking up a few dollars serving on juries. Eventually he landed the job of postmaster of New Salem. The mail was delivered to New Salem once a week. Residents were supposed to pick up their mail from the post office. When they didn't, Lincoln often put the letters in his hat and delivered them personally.

Being postmaster didn't fill up his time or pay enough to support himself, so he continued taking odd jobs. He got his next break when the general surveyor, a man Lincoln had served with in the Black Hawk War, offered him the job of assistant surveyor. Lincoln eagerly accepted. He purchased a compass, found a book on surveying, and set to work. Surveying was difficult. It required hacking through briar patches and undergrowth and slogging through swamps to measure the land. He often returned from a day of surveying with scratches and torn clothing, but he shrugged it off. The rapid arrival of new settlers meant that he had steady work.

About this time, Henry Clay and a few others who were opposed to the Democrats formed a new political party called the Whigs. The new party favored a strong national bank and federally funded improvements. The Whigs also wanted to restrict voting to those who owned property in the hopes of making sure the voters were well-informed and invested in the laws. As a result, Jacksonian Democrats scoffed at the Whigs as a party of bankers, wealthy merchants, and aristocratic East Coast families. For Lincoln, though, the Whig party stood for progress and growth. Lincoln believed that what made America the envy of the world was that

the self-made man was a reality. He saw the Whigs as the party that made it possible for an enterprising man to rise from poverty. Many Whigs were antislavery, recognizing that slavery made a lie of the claim that *any* man in America could rise as high as his abilities allowed.

Lincoln joined the Whig Party as soon as it was formed and became a devoted and enthusias-

Henry Clay, founder of the Whig Party, published by N. Currier, between 1835 and 1856

tic party member. Becoming involved with the party allowed him to widen his circle of friends beyond New Salem.

By the time the next elections came around in 1834, Lincoln felt ready to run once more for office. He campaigned on the need to build a canal from the inland farming areas to the Sangamon River. The canal he wanted to build would prevent flooding in the spring and allow farmers to transport their produce forty miles away to the Illinois River with access to world markets. He was careful not to criticize the wildly popular Andrew Jackson. Except for talking about how the canal would benefit *all* residents of the region, his campaign was "more of a hand-shaking campaign than anything else."

He didn't hesitate to earn votes by living up to local ideas of what made a strong candidate. At one campaign stop, a group of Democrats offered a challenge. "See here Lincoln," one of them said, "if you can throw this cannon ball farther than we can, we'll vote for you." Lincoln threw the cannon ball farther than any of the others—and won all their votes. At another stop, a friend and supporter introduced him to a few men working in a field. One of the men declared that he would "not vote for a man unless he could make a hand." Lincoln said, "If that is all, I am sure of your votes." He took the cradle used for harvesting grain and expertly did a round of the entire field. The men were impressed with Lincoln's physical strength. Lincoln "didn't lose a single vote in the crowd."

Lincoln never hid his beliefs, even the ones that were largely unpopular. He stated his political views so calmly and humbly that people who disagreed with him were not offended. Because he was so calm and straightforward with his views, he struck people as honest with no hidden motives. One of Lincoln's former customers from his store, a Democrat and Jackson supporter, explained, "I voted for Lincoln in opposition to my own creed and faith in politics." Lincoln won the support of Whigs who agreed with him and Democrats who liked him personally.

This time when the votes were counted, Lincoln placed second in a field of thirteen candidates, trailing the first-place winner by only fourteen votes. He thus became one of four representatives to the State Assembly. The term of service was two years. He prepared for his new job by reading law books and borrowing money to buy a suit—the first he ever owned. On an autumn day in 1834, at the age of twenty-five, he climbed into a stagecoach and set out for Vandalia, the capital of Illinois.

✶ ✶ ✶ ✶ ✶ ✶ ✶ ✶ ✶ ✶ ✶ ✶ ✶ ✶ ✶

Lincoln roomed in one of Vandalia's boardinghouses with other legislators. The statehouse where the Assembly met was a dilapidated two-story building with bulging walls. Chunks of plaster occasionally fell on the statesmen. Lincoln spent his first session mostly listening and learning, feeling awed by his fellow representatives, many of whom were accomplished lawyers.

One of the legislators who roomed in the same boardinghouse as Lincoln was a lawyer from Springfield named John T. Stuart. Lincoln and Stuart had served together in the Black Hawk War. Stuart encouraged Lincoln to study law and lent him law books. Lincoln studied diligently under Stuart's guidance and became so skilled at drawing up legislation that his colleagues turned to him to draft the bills. It was evident to Lincoln's contemporaries that he loved politics. According to one friend and colleague, Lincoln "reveled in [politics], as a fish does in water, as a bird disports itself on the sustaining air."

✶ ✶ ✶ ✶ ✶ ✶ ✶ ✶ ✶ ✶ ✶ ✶ ✶ ✶ ✶

When the first session ended, Lincoln returned to New Salem and resumed his job as surveyor. With his burgeoning self-confidence, he set his sights on becoming a lawyer. At the time there were only seven law schools in the United States and none in Illinois. Therefore, the way to become a lawyer was to study with lawyers, and then pass an exam. Lincoln devoured the leading law texts: Joseph Chitty's *Precedents in Pleading*, Joseph Story's *Commentaries on Equity Jurisprudence*, and William

Blackstone's *Commentaries on the Laws of England*. He found his copy of Blackstone's *Commentaries* at the bottom of a barrel of rubbish. "I began to read those famous works," Lincoln said, "and I had plenty of time; for, during the long summer days when the farmers were busy with their crops, my customers were few and far between. The more I read, the more intensely interested I became. Never in my whole life was my mind so thoroughly absorbed."

Friends were amused by his reading habits. He often sat barefoot, leaning against a tree or lying on his back and propping his long legs against the trunk. He moved as the sun moved, circling around the tree to remain in the shade, so absorbed in his books that he didn't hear people walking by. When acquaintances greeted him, they were met with silence.

That summer, he fell in love with Ann Mayes Rutledge, the daughter of community leader James Rutledge. Lincoln was painfully shy around women, but he felt at ease with Ann, and she warmed up to the clumsy man with a Kentucky twang. Not much is known about Lincoln's relationship with Ann Rutledge, other than that they had an understanding that they would marry when he became a lawyer and could support a wife. Ann's sister Nancy later reported that Lincoln "declared his love and was

44

accepted . . . No one could have seen them together and not be convinced that they loved each other truly."

Later in the summer, typhoid fever raged through Illinois, and Ann fell victim. The doctors prescribed absolute quiet, but she insisted on seeing Lincoln. She died a few days after their visit, leaving Lincoln devastated. He fell into a deep depression. A local resident recalled that, "his gloom seemed to deepen for some time, so as to give anxiety to his friends in regard to his mind." After being stricken with grief for months, he pulled himself from his emotional abyss by plunging back into his law books. This was to become a pattern all his life: Whenever he became paralyzed with melancholy or grief, he would lift himself from his depression through study and work.

He spent his second year in the Assembly like his first—mostly listening and learning. In 1836, after concluding his second session in the Assembly and meeting the requirements to become a lawyer, he received his license to practice law for the Illinois Supreme Court. He also decided to run for reelection. During the previous elections, he had confined himself to the rural towns and districts where he had friends and felt comfortable. Now a lawyer and experienced legislator, he had the confidence to venture into the larger towns and cities like Springfield, where he shook hands and gave speeches. During his first moments in front of a large crowd, he appeared ill at ease, often stuffing his fists into his pockets. But as he warmed to his subject, his timidity fell away, and he impressed his audiences as a capable and good-humored speaker. This time he took on the Democrats directly, accusing them of blocking improvements in Illinois and thus harming the hardworking people.

When the votes were counted, he finished first in a field of seventeen, remarkable given that Democrats held a commanding majority in Illinois. During his third year in the Assembly, he took a more active role. He and other Whigs joined with the Democrats to help fund two major railroad lines through the state and build a canal linking the Illinois River with the Michigan Canal—a canal that might have become as important as the Erie Canal in opening up backwoods areas to trade and commerce. The passage of the bill was greeted with joyous celebrations. Townspeople cheered and lit bonfires in the streets. The future of Illinois seemed bright.

Then came the financial panic of 1837, the worst economic depression thus far in the nation's history. The Whigs blamed the depression on former president Jackson's decision to kill the Second Bank of the United States. When Jackson shut down the national bank, he ordered all federal funds moved to state banks. The problem was that state banks, not properly regulated, engaged in reckless speculation, lending out too much money to people who were unable to pay. When borrowers were unable to repay their loans, the banks ran out of funds and shut down, causing customers who had deposited money in the banks to lose everything. People lost their homes, farms, and lifetime savings. The value of land plunged and entire communities throughout the nation turned into ghost towns. The State of Illinois was forced to abandon its plans for railroads and canals.

The Times, by Edward Williams Clay, published by H. R. Robinson, 1837. Illustration shows the financial panic of 1837, with people begging in the streets.

Jackson supporters didn't blame Jackson's bank policies for the financial crisis. They placed the blame on politicians like Lincoln who had pushed for publicly funded improvements, claiming that any government spending was reckless and took money from the pockets of the citizens, thus creating financial hardships for everyone.

Despite the collapse of his plans for building a canal, Lincoln was able to achieve some success as a legislator when he led an effort to move the Illinois capital from Vandalia to Springfield, a larger and more centrally located town. Vandalia was in the south, where the state was mostly rural and Democratic. The move to Springfield would help the Whigs, whose interest lay more in the northern, industrial part of the state. Lincoln argued that Springfield's central location would allow the state government to better represent the entire state.

Lincoln introduced the bill and shepherded it through the legislature, a process that honed his political skills. Twice the bill was abandoned, and twice Lincoln brought it back to life by offering compromises, including requiring Springfield to pay for the necessary buildings.

On February 25, 1837, the legislature approved the bill, making Lincoln a hero in Springfield. That evening, Lincoln and others celebrated at Ebenezer Capps's tavern and invited all the legislators to attend. Ninian Edwards, the wealthy son of a former governor and a resident of Springfield, footed the bill for oysters, almonds, raisins, and other delicacies. Lincoln was the toast of the party.

✳ ✳ ✳ ✳ ✳ ✳ ✳ ✳ ✳ ✳ ✳ ✳ ✳ ✳ ✳

Slavery, the most hotly debated and divisive issue of the day, burst into Illinois politics during Lincoln's second term in the Assembly, when the American Anti-Slavery Society started a massive petition to outlaw slavery in the District of Columbia. The petition unleashed a nationwide debate over whether Congress had the authority to abolish slavery in Washington, D.C.

The Southern slaveholding states joined to oppose the petition. Members of the Illinois Assembly, to show solidarity with the Southern states, introduced a resolution criticizing the American Anti-Slavery Society and promising to help protect slavery in the District of Columbia. According to the resolution, the State of Illinois disapproved of abolitionist groups and agreed with the South that the right to own slaves was sacred. When the votes were counted, seventy-seven Illinois lawmakers supported the proslavery resolution. Lincoln and five other legislators opposed it.

Antislavery activists like Lincoln faced an uphill battle, not only because they were in the minority, but because the U.S. Constitution—the highest law in the land—protected the rights of slave owners.

Half the states allowed for slavery, so abolitionists knew they had no chance of getting enough votes in Congress to amend the Constitution to outlaw slavery. Frustrated, leading abolitionist

The framers of the U.S. Constitution compromised over the issue of slavery. One of the compromises was to count slaves as three-fifths of a person. Article IV, Section 2, the so-called Fugitive Slave Clause, required runaways to be returned to their masters. According to Founding Father Alexander Hamilton, without such compromises no union could have possibly been formed, because the Southern states would not have joined if slavery were forbidden.

While the Constitution allowed slavery, the Constitution also allowed for the control and abolition of slavery. Section 9 of Article I of the Constitution allowed Congress to regulate the migration of slaves after 1808. Moreover, at any time the Constitution could be amended—as long as two-thirds of both houses of

William Lloyd Garrison scandalized the nation when, in front of an audience, he burned a copy of the Constitution and declared it an evil document. Other abolitionists called for violent slave revolts, leading many Southerners to believe that abolitionism was an evil plot intended to bring about the wholesale slaughter of Southern whites.

Congress approved of the changes and the changes were ratified by three-fourths of the states.

Both the proslavery and the antislavery sides argued that the Fifth Amendment of the Constitution supported their positions. The Fifth Amendment prevents the federal government from taking away a citizen's "life, liberty, or property" without due process of law—meaning fair legal procedures must be followed. Slave owners, counting those enslaved as property, claimed that the Fifth Amendment forbade the federal government to interfere with their property right in slaves. The antislavery side, counting those enslaved as people, claimed that blacks had the right to liberty under the Fifth Amendment.

Masthead for William Lloyd Garrison's abolitionist newspaper, *The Liberator*, by Charles Howland Hammatt Billings, 1850

Slaveholders painted *all* abolitionists as Constitution-hating, unlawful, and un-American. They argued that slave owners were the true patriots, revering the Constitution as it was handed down by the Founding Fathers. They also argued that the principles of democracy meant that whatever a majority of voters wanted, the majority should get. With only white males allowed to vote, they knew slavery would win majorities throughout the South.

Lincoln feared that some of the methods used by the abolitionists made matters worse instead of better. Lincoln also believed that laws must be respected as long as they were in place. He looked to the Declaration of Independence—which stated that all men were created equal—as capturing the ideals and intentions of the Founding Fathers. He believed the Constitution needed to be interpreted in a way that brought it in line with the noble ideal that *all* men were created equal.

✭ ✭ ✭ ✭ ✭ ✭ ✭ ✭ ✭ ✭ ✭ ✭ ✭ ✭ ✭

On March 3, 1837, six weeks after the Illinois lawmakers approved the resolution denouncing abolitionism and defending slavery in the District of Columbia, Lincoln wrote a protest against the resolution in which he said that "the institution of slavery is founded on both injustice and bad policy" and was "abhorrent to the ideas and true meaning of the Constitution." Lincoln responded to the argument that in a democracy the majority of voters should have what they wanted by saying no, democracy doesn't mean *majority rules*, it means *all* people have the right to liberty and the pursuit of happiness.

The only other member of the Assembly who would join Lincoln in signing the protest was Daniel Stone, an assemblyman who was not afraid to put forward an unpopular opinion because he was not seeking reelection. When Lincoln drafted his protest and stood almost alone against the proslavery majority, he demonstrated once again the stubbornness that led him to rebel against his father's efforts to stop him from reading. While Lincoln had a knack for sensing the needs of others and accommodating himself, he was also capable of standing firm with a quiet tenacity when he believed he was right.

The Jacksonian Democrats believed that democracy meant majority rule in all matters. John Adams, America's second president, pointed out the problem with majority rule in all matters: There would be nothing to prevent the majority from passing laws that brutalized the minority—a concept President Adams called the tyranny of the majority.

The Founding Fathers understood that too much democracy could lead to mob rule—a prospect that frightened them. Alexander Hamilton famously said that the purpose of government was to constrain unruly passions and compel people to conform to the dictates of reason. The Constitution—with its checks, balances, and protections for individual rights—was designed to protect individual liberty by limiting the power of majority rule.

Lincoln insisted that democracy meant that all people were entitled to equal treatment and equal opportunities for advancement.

Mary Todd

*I have come to the conclusion never again
to think of marrying, and for this reason, I can
never be satisfied with anyone who would
be blockhead enough to have me.*

— Abraham Lincoln

hen Lincoln's third legislative session ended, he returned to New Salem, but he didn't plan to stay. Without the improvements New Salem desperately needed, the river had become too treacherous for steamboats, and as a result, the town was failing. With residents moving away to more prosperous towns, New Salem was turning into a ghost town unable to support a law practice. John Stuart, Lincoln's friend and colleague from the Assembly who had guided his legal studies,

invited Lincoln to become a partner in his Springfield law office.

Lincoln accepted the offer. He arrived in Springfield on April 15, 1837, with all his possessions—a few law books and some clothing—in his saddlebags. For a man like Lincoln, accustomed to backcountry villages, Springfield was a major urban center, but by East Coast sensibilities, the new capital of Illinois was still a frontier town. While there were a few brick mansions, the buildings were mostly log cabins. The town was dusty and shabby, with hogs and chickens roaming the streets.

Lincoln was no stranger to his new hometown. He had given speeches in Springfield and was a minor celebrity for having played an important role in moving the capital there. On his first day in town, he met Joshua Speed, who would become a lifelong friend. Speed owned a store and lived above it. He had heard Lincoln give a speech once and knew him by reputation. When Lincoln entered Speed's store to make some purchases, the two men got to talking and hit it off. Seeing that Lincoln needed a place to live, Speed invited him to share his living quarters.

Lincoln spent his days practicing law, handling a variety of cases—divorces, trespass, probate, and criminal matters, basically anything that came his way. During his first years in law practice, most of his cases were of small importance. One was a dispute over who was the owner of a litter of pigs, and another over who was to blame for the loss of a flock of sheep.

In the evenings, Lincoln gathered with other men around the fire in Speed's store. They read newspapers and discussed politics. As in New Salem, Lincoln was well liked for his good humor and storytelling. He would say, "That reminds me of a story," and launch into whatever anecdote he was reminded of. Some of his listeners questioned whether he was making his stories up on the spot because they fit so well into the conversation. After Lincoln arrived in Springfield, the group in Speed's store grew larger, with people coming because they were sure to find Lincoln.

Serving in the Assembly was much more convenient now for Lincoln. Like Stuart, he could keep up his law practice, thereby enabling himself to earn a decent living. By his fourth session in the Assembly, he was one of the more experienced legislators. He became a leader of the Whigs, and served on fourteen committees, including the influential finance committee. He confidently took the floor to engage in debates.

He did not seek reelection when his fourth term ended, though. The nation's financial crisis had doomed any hope of internal improvements in Illinois. Instead of running for office, he threw himself into Whig Party business. To promote Whig politics, he organized voters and coordinated rallies and fairs. He campaigned on behalf of Whig candidates, gave speeches, and wrote letters for publication in the newspaper.

With his gift for making friends, he was soon moving in the highest social circles in Springfield. Among the mansions in which he was a regular guest was one owned by Elizabeth Todd Edwards and her husband, Ninian Edwards. Edwards was a staunch Whig, but he invited all the town's prominent citizens to his gatherings, including Stephen Douglas, a leader of the local Democrats, and a man who would one day become Lincoln's political rival.

Elizabeth Todd Edwards had an unmarried sister named Mary, who came to live with her. Lincoln met Mary Todd one Sunday at a party at the Edwards home, and he was instantly captivated. Mary had soft brown hair, blue eyes, and a bright, intelligent face. The daughter of a wealthy lawyer and businessman, she was cultured, charming, and flirtatious. She was also capable of being sharp and sarcastic. In a time when few women had formal educations, Mary had been educated at the finest girl's academies, where she'd been a gifted student. She had grown up in a political household. Henry Clay was a close family friend. Her father, a Whig spokesman in Kentucky, referred to the politics of Andrew Jackson as "Locofoco." He hoped that one day a Whig president would crumble Locofoco to dust. Mary herself had a keen interest in current events and harbored a secret wish to be the wife of a U.S. president.

Mary Todd Lincoln, by Nicholas Shepherd, 1846 or 1847, about four years after she and Lincoln were married

After Mary's arrival in Springfield, she became the belle of the town. She was happiest when she was surrounded by friends. Among her admirers was Stephen Douglas.

Mary Todd was exactly the kind of young woman who left Lincoln shy and tongue-tied. As Mary's sister Elizabeth said of Lincoln, he "could not hold a lengthy conversation with a lady . . . he was not sufficiently educated and intelligent in the female line." To make matters worse, Lincoln was a terrible dancer, which he explained once by saying, "My feet weren't made that way." Ordinarily at parties he avoided the dance floor, preferring to gather with a group of men who he could entertain with jokes and stories. But he summoned the courage to ask Mary to dance, telling her, "I want to dance with you the worst way." After they danced, she said, "Mr. Lincoln, I think you have literally fulfilled your request—you have danced the worst way possible."

Of all her admirers, Mary favored Lincoln. Elizabeth Edwards believed that Mary "flirted with Douglas in order to spur up Lincoln to a greater love." To help Lincoln past his awkwardness, Mary "led the conversation . . . Lincoln would listen and gaze on her as if drawn by some superior power, irresistibly so; he listened, never scarcely said a word." Later, when Mary discussed Lincoln with a friend, she dismissed his homely rawboned appearance and awkwardness by saying, "But I mean to make him the president of the United States all the same. You will see that, as I always told you, I will yet be the president's wife."

Mary and Lincoln were opposites in appearance as well as manners. She was small and plump, he tall and cadaverous. Lively, talkative, and passionate, Mary was "impulsive & made no attempt to conceal her feeling, indeed it would have been an impossibility had she desired to do so, for her face was an index to every passing emotion." Lincoln, in contrast, was slow moving, often melancholy, and given to long silences. Nonetheless, they had much in common. Both were from Kentucky, both loved poetry and politics, and both admired Henry Clay.

Ninian and Elizabeth Edwards recognized Lincoln as a man with a bright future, and encouraged a match between him and

Mary. Within a few months, Lincoln and Mary were engaged—but then something went wrong. Lincoln had second thoughts. He doubted his ability to support a wife. He doubted whether he was enough in love with Mary. He was also uncertain about marriage in general. Lincoln's quip that he could never be satisfied with anyone blockheaded enough to have him may have held a great deal of truth, offering a window into the mind of a man genuinely conflicted about marriage. Matters were not helped when Lincoln found himself suddenly attracted to another relative of Ninian Edwards, a young woman named Matilda Edwards.

Initially he planned to write Mary a letter calling off the engagement, but Joshua Speed persuaded him to break the news in person. So Lincoln visited Mary at her sister's house. When he told her that he wanted to break off their engagement, she burst into tears. Afterward she pulled herself together and wrote him a letter releasing him.

Instead of feeling relieved to receive the letter, he was devastated. Nothing came of his attraction to Matilda Edwards, and almost immediately after receiving Mary's letter, he regretted his decision. He felt guilty for causing Mary pain. He stopped attending parties at the Edwards mansion. Questioning his ability to "keep [his] resolves when they are made," he sank into so deep a depression that he was completely immobilized. He told his partner John Stuart, "I am now the most miserable man living. If what I feel were equally distributed to the whole human family, there would not be one cheerful face on the earth." Acquaintances, seeing his deep melancholy, concluded that Mary had rejected him.

Meanwhile Mary missed Lincoln, writing to a friend that she had been "much alone of late . . . [Lincoln] deems me unworthy of notice, as I have not met him in this [world] for months." With remarkable insight into his character, she understood that if she waited, he'd be back. Meanwhile Lincoln, who knew how to work through his bouts of melancholy, told Speed that in such times it was crucial to avoid being idle, for keeping busy would "rest from that intensity of thought which will sometimes wear the sweetest idea threadbare and turn it to the bitterness of death."

About this time, John Stuart and Lincoln ended their law partnership, and Lincoln formed a partnership with Stephen T. Logan, a prominent Whig whose grandfather had been elected the first State Treasurer of Kentucky. Lincoln's legal work kept him busy enough so that as summer approached, he was able to pull himself from his depression.

Lincoln tried to resume his relationship with Mary, but now

Elizabeth and Ninian Edwards were against him. Seeing how Lincoln had handled the engagement, Ninian concluded Lincoln was "crazy as a loon." Elizabeth was convinced that Lincoln and Mary were too different in temperament to be happy together.

When Mary and Lincoln began seeing each other again, they hid their meetings from Ninian and Elizabeth. Lincoln proposed once more, and once more Mary accepted him. They announced they would be married immediately. Elizabeth Edwards later told an interviewer she had only a few hours' notice. Without time to bake a cake, she had to send for one in town.

No sooner did Lincoln make the announcement, he was again tormented by second thoughts. This time he kept his doubts mostly to himself. Shortly before the wedding, however, he almost lost his nerve. When a little boy, seeing him all dressed up, asked where he was going, he said, "To hell, I suppose." A good friend recalled that he looked and acted as if he were going to the slaughter. But the wedding itself went forward without a hitch. The ceremony was held the evening of November 4, 1842, in the parlor of the Edwards' mansion. The couple said their vows in the lovely light of gas lamps while a fire crackled in the nearby fireplace. Outside, a soft rain was falling. The ring Lincoln slipped onto Mary's finger was engraved with the words "Love is eternal."

A Practical Statesman

A drop of honey catches more flies
than a gallon of gall. So with men.
If you would win a man to your cause,
first convince him that you are
his sincere friend.

— Abraham Lincoln

incoln's marriage meant he was now connected to one of the most prominent families in Kentucky. Some of Lincoln's acquaintances even speculated that part of his attraction to Mary was that her connections could help him advance. Members of Mary's wealthy, slave-owning family believed she had married beneath her. Mary herself disapproved of many of Lincoln's backcountry manners. She complained that he ate butter with a knife, that he didn't care if his cuffs were frayed, and that he often forgot about engagements.

Right away she began schooling him in the social graces expected of those at the top of the social ladder. Lincoln responded by ignoring her or making jokes—but eventually his manners and clothing *did* improve.

The newlyweds rented a room on the second floor of a boarding-house called the Globe Tavern. Lincoln wanted to run for Congress, and Mary strongly encouraged him to do so. Statewide election was difficult for a Whig, but he could run for U.S. congressman from the Seventh Congressional District, which included Springfield—a district with a large Whig population and where he had many friends and supporters. During the winter of 1842–1843, he set out to win the Whig nomination. Some of Lincoln's friends believed he ran for Congress only because Mary was "pushing him on in his ambition" and "nagging her husband on." Mary's sister Elizabeth confirmed that Mary was the most ambitious woman she knew, and that she spurred up Lincoln, encouraging him to seize his opportunities.

Lincoln, however, made clear he *wanted* to be a congressman. "Now if you should hear anyone say that Lincoln don't want to go to Congress," he told a fellow lawyer and Whig leader, "I wish you as a personal friend of mine would tell him you have reason to believe he is mistaken. The truth is, I would like very much to go."

His two rivals for the Whig nomination were both friends: John J. Hardin and Edward Baker. John Hardin was also Mary's third cousin. In March, the Sangamon County Whigs met to choose their candidate. Early on in the voting, it appeared that Baker had a commanding lead. At about noon, several people asked Lincoln to withdraw because Baker was so far ahead of him. Lincoln accommodated the request. Later it was discovered that Baker's lead was much smaller than people had thought. Baker supporters had cleverly arranged for the earliest votes to be those for Baker so he would appear to have a commanding lead. Learning of this, Mary was furious because she believed Lincoln had given up too easily.

★ ★ ★ ★ ★ ★ ★ ★ ★ ★ ★ ★ ★ ★

On August 3, 1843, the Lincolns' first child, a boy, was born. Lincoln joked that he was afraid their son might have one of his long legs and one of Mary's short ones, and would thus have a terrible time getting through the world. They named their son Robert Todd for Mary's father, and called him Bobbie.

Now that they were a family of three, the Lincolns moved to a rented frame house on South Fourth Street. The following year, they bought a home of their own on the corner of Eighth and

Jackson—a sturdy, well-built house. Later they added a second floor with two more bedrooms and a loft for storage. Their home was a short walk from Lincoln's law office.

Mary spent her time at home caring for Bobbie and the house. She followed the custom of Springfield housewives of devoting Wednesdays and Saturdays to baking and Mondays and Tuesdays to washing and ironing. She delegated much of the washing and ironing to hired servants. Lincoln meanwhile spent long hours at his office. He was moving up in the legal community, representing corporate clients with more complex cases.

When the Lincolns first bought their home in 1856, it had only one story. Pictured here is the Lincoln home after they enlarged it to accommodate their growing family. Lincoln is in the yard with his sons William ("Willie") and Thomas ("Tad"). Photographed by John Adams Whipple, 1860.

He studied diligently and became a master at the fine points of procedure and law. "When I have a particular case in hand," he said, "I love to dig up the question by the roots and hold it up and dry it before the fires of the mind." His work as a lawyer allowed him to further improve his public speaking skills. He learned how to make an emotional connection with a jury, making each juror feel that he was talking directly to him.

★ ★ ★ ★ ★ ★ ★ ★ ★ ★ ★ ★ ★ ★

The 1844 presidential election pitted Whig Henry Clay against Democrat James Knox Polk. The election promised to be a close one. One of the dividing issues was whether to annex Texas.

For decades, American settlers had been pushing into the region of Mexico north of the Rio Grande into what is now Texas, bringing enslaved workers with them. Initially the Mexican government invited the settlers into the area, but then Mexico outlawed slavery in 1828, which caused trouble between the Mexican authorities and the slave-owning Americans, who refused to free their slaves.

In 1836, Texas declared independence from Mexico. Sam Houston led an army against the Mexican government. After the

Texans suffered a tragic defeat at the Alamo, they regrouped, won their independence, and established the Republic of Texas. That same year, Texans applied for statehood.

Sam Houston, by Mathew Brady, between 1848 and 1850

At the time, about fifteen percent of the population of Texas were "free people of color." The new Constitution of Texas, though, included the statement that "No free person of African descent, either in whole or in part, shall be permitted to reside permanently in the Republic of Texas without the consent of Congress." Many free blacks nonetheless remained in Texas, but they were subjected to brutal laws that at times forced them to work and even submit to branding. The government encouraged them to go back into slavery by allowing freed blacks to choose their own masters. The population of enslaved men and women grew rapidly after Texas won its independence. Initially there were about five thousand slaves in Texas. By the eve of the Civil War, the enslaved population swelled to more than 185,000.

Battle of the Alamo, by Percy Moran, 1910

Democratic candidate Polk dreamed of the United States spanning the entire continent and was strongly in favor of annexing Texas. Abolitionists, though, were against admitting Texas to the Union because they didn't want to add another slave state. Whigs generally opposed annexing Texas, but they didn't speak out strongly against it. Whigs instead built their campaign around their support for a new national bank, internal improvements, and government regulations to help industry and business.

Lincoln campaigned for Clay. Among the places Lincoln was invited to speak was Rockport, Indiana. He accepted the invitation and for the first time returned to his childhood home in Indiana. He was speaking in Rockport when in the crowd he saw one of his childhood friends, Nathaniel Grigsby. At the conclusion of his speech, the two men greeted each other. They returned to the boardinghouse where Lincoln was staying, and spent the evening reminiscing about their childhoods.

The next day, with Grigsby, Lincoln revisited his boyhood home and the place where his mother and sister were buried. Lincoln, who rarely expressed emotions to others, poured his feelings into a poem, which began with:

My childhood's home I see again
And sadden with the view;
And still, as memory crowds my brain,
There's pleasure in it too.

✴ ✴ ✴ ✴ ✴ ✴ ✴ ✴ ✴ ✴ ✴ ✴ ✴ ✴ ✴

The Democrats campaigned on a platform of repealing the Missouri Compromise so that there would be no limits on the spread of slavery into the territories.

In 1819, when Missouri applied for statehood, James Tallmadge, a congressman from Poughkeepsie, New York, proposed that as a condition of Missouri statehood, slavery in Missouri must be prohibited. His proposal created a firestorm of debate over whether Congress had the authority under the Constitution to prevent the spread of slavery into new states and territories.

The Missouri debate was resolved in what came to be

It soon became clear that Whig Henry Clay would lose to Democrat James Polk. The problem was that the Whig Party was crumbling over the issue of slavery.

The Whigs divided into the "Conscience Whigs" of the North who opposed slavery and the "Cotton Whigs" of the South, like Henry Clay, who were slave owners but opposed the spread of slavery into the territories. Many of the Conscience Whigs refused to vote for Clay because he was a slave owner, instead throwing their support behind Liberty Party candidate James G. Birney, thereby splitting the anti-Democrat vote. As a result, proslavery Polk carried New York, which gave him enough support to win nationwide and become president.

called the Missouri Compromise: To keep the slave and free states balanced, Missouri was admitted as a slave state and Maine as a free state, with slavery forever banned in territories west and north of Missouri. The Missouri Compromise didn't really please anyone. Southerners were angry at the very idea that Congress could make laws limiting slavery, and abolitionists were alarmed that slavery was spreading to the territories and new states.

Because of the constitutional protections for slavery, Lincoln believed the only way to end slavery was to stop its spread into the territories. Lincoln reasoned that when free states vastly outnumbered slave states, the institution of slavery would eventually collapse because it would no longer have widespread support. Slave owners similarly understood that the only way to preserve slavery was to allow slavery in the new territories. Should the day come when free states far outnumbered slave states, it would be an easy matter for the majority of states to amend the Constitution and outlaw slavery. Thus the question of whether slaves should be permitted into the territories was the most fiercely debated issue of the day.

One Conscience Whig who defected to the Liberty Party confronted Lincoln over his vote for Clay, telling him that people of conscience shouldn't vote for a slave owner. The Conscience Whig insisted that a vote for a slave owner was a vote for evil. Lincoln replied, "If by your votes you could have prevented the extension of slavery, would it have been good and not evil so to have used your votes, even though it involved casting of them for a slaveholder? By the fruit the tree is to be known. An evil tree cannot bring forth good fruit. If the fruit of electing Mr. Clay would have been to prevent the extension of slavery, could the act of electing have been evil?"

Lincoln was devastated by Clay's defeat. He placed the blame squarely on the Northern Whigs who defected to the Liberty Party. Some of Lincoln's friends and acquaintances were so distressed over the election of another proslavery president that they were ready to give up on politics altogether. In the words of David Davis, a Springfield lawyer, "Clay's defeat weaned me from politics . . . There is precious little use for any Whig in Illinois to be wasting his time and efforts. This state cannot be redeemed." Some in New England wanted to secede from the Union because they didn't want to be part of a slave-owning nation.

Congressman Lincoln

Our government rests in public opinion.
Whoever can change public opinion,
can change the government.

— Abraham Lincoln

ot long after the election, Stephen Logan wanted to go into partnership with his son, so Lincoln again found himself without a law partner. Lincoln was by then at the top of the legal profession in Springfield, so he could have had his pick of partners. To the surprise of his colleagues, he selected William H. Herndon, a young and inexperienced lawyer. He and Herndon had met when Herndon was in a crowd listening to Lincoln speak. Herndon was "halooing for him," when Lincoln called to him, asked his name,

and said, "So you are a good Whig, eh?" Later Lincoln guided him through his legal studies. When Logan left the partnership, Lincoln sought out Herndon, who hadn't yet taken his exam, and asked him if he wanted to enter a law partnership. At first Herndon thought Lincoln was joking.

William Herndon at about age fifty-seven, photographer unknown, circa 1878

When he understood Lincoln was serious, he stammered out his acceptance, saying, "It is an undeserved honor, and yet I say I will gladly and thankfully accept the kind and generous offer."

Herndon moved into Lincoln's law offices. As the senior partner, Lincoln interviewed clients, wrote the more important legal documents, and made most of the court appearances. Herndon performed the routine office tasks and legal research. Despite the differences in their expertise and experience, Lincoln insisted on splitting all profits equally. Neither Lincoln nor Herndon was particularly organized or neat, so they were constantly searching for missing documents. In one corner of the office was a stack of papers. On top was a note in Lincoln's handwriting that said, "When you can't find it anywhere else, look in this."

✻ ✻ ✻ ✻ ✻ ✻ ✻ ✻ ✻ ✻ ✻ ✻ ✻ ✻ ✻

The Lincolns' second son was born on March 10, 1846. They named him Edward Baker after a good friend of Lincoln's—the same Edward Baker who had beaten Lincoln for the Whig congressional nomination two years earlier. Lincoln was determined that his children would not resent him the way he resented his own father, so he wanted no "parental tyranny" in his home. Mary, too, was an indulgent mother. Contrary to the norms of the day, which approved of spankings and strict discipline, the Lincolns believed children should grow up without a battery of rules and restrictions. The result was that friends and neighbors believed the Lincolns spoiled their children. One observer said the boys literally ran over Lincoln, who was "powerless to withstand their importunities."

After a long day at work, Lincoln would come home, pick up a book, and sit in front of the fire. Mary, who was more energetic and sociable, craved conversation. After spending all day caring for the boys and the house, she felt frustrated when her quiet and moody husband paid no attention to her. She grew short-tempered and demanding, which in turn caused Lincoln to withdraw further. Lincoln often went for long walks alone, and lingered when he traveled to distant courts. Bobby's early memories of his father were watching his father pack his saddlebags before heading out to make faraway appearances. Lincoln's long absences made Mary even more irritable.

One day Lincoln told a friend that Mary had been in a "tirade so fierce" that he "pushed her through the door" and shouted, "if you can't stop this abuse, damn you, get out." The consensus of the neighbors and Lincoln's friends was that Mary's personality was the cause of the Lincolns' marital problems. Some of Lincoln's friends believed that Lincoln entered politics to have an excuse to get out of his house. They believed that if Mary had made their home more serene and inviting—as a nineteenth century wife was supposed to do—Lincoln would have wanted to stay home more instead of running for office. At the same time, Lincoln's friends admitted that the inward and melancholy Lincoln, who rarely expressed his personal feelings or emotions, could not have been an easy man to live with.

Despite the friction in their marriage and the differences in their personalities, much bound them together. Both loved politics. Both doted on their children. And both had high ambitions for Lincoln's political future.

* * * * * * * * * * * * * * *

When the next elections rolled around in 1846, Lincoln once more ran for Congress. He launched his campaign quietly, writing letters to influential Whigs and meeting with his wide circle of acquaintances.

America at the time was undergoing rapid expansion. After Texas joined the Union as a slave state, President Polk started a border war with Mexico, hoping to expand American holdings. Polk's Mexican War resulted in the Treaty of Guadalupe Hidalgo, bringing under control of the United States the vast Western territory that would eventually become California, Nevada, Utah, Arizona, Colorado, New Mexico, and parts of Wyoming, Oklahoma, Colorado, Kansas, and Montana. Meanwhile, with American pioneers flocking to the Pacific Northwest by way of the Oregon Trail, President Polk signed the Oregon Treaty with Great Britain, acquiring territory that would become the future states of Oregon, Washington, Idaho, and parts of Wyoming and Montana.

Each new territory sparked fresh debates over the expansion of slavery, with abolitionists decrying the spread of an immoral institution, and those who were proslavery insisting that forbidding slavery in the territories would unconstitutionally deny Southerners the right to move into American-held territories with their "property."

Lincoln remained quiet about the Democratic expansionism, focusing his campaign instead on the issues dear to the Whigs: internal improvements and tariffs (taxes on imports designed to protect American manufacturers). His strategy for winning the Whig nomination was simple. He praised his opponent, incumbent John Hardin, as talented and energetic, adding simply that, "Turn about is fair play." He was the party workhorse. For years he had been helping Whigs get elected. Now it was his turn.

His strategy was surprisingly effective. Because of his dedication to the party and his wide circle of friends, enough people agreed that it was his turn to represent his district in Congress.

Once it was clear that Lincoln would win the Whig nomination, Hardin saved face by dropping out. When the votes in the final election were counted, Lincoln won a seat in the U.S. House of Representatives with more than 55 percent of the vote.

Abraham Lincoln, frontier lawyer and congressman-elect at age thirty-seven, by Nicholas H. Shepherd, 1846 or 1847. He didn't grow a beard until after he was elected president.

Mary was thrilled by the idea of living in Washington, D.C. Because the next session would not begin until December of 1847, they had almost a year and a half to get ready for their move and find a renter for their home. When the time came to travel to Washington, Lincoln, Mary, and their two boys first visited Mary's family in Kentucky, and then traveled by train to Washington, arriving in time for the opening of the Congressional session in December.

The nation's capital consisted of broad avenues lined with hotels and shops surrounded by wide expanses of open fields with a scattering of houses. The Lincolns spent their first few days at the Indian Queen, a small hotel on Pennsylvania Avenue. After that they rented a room in a boardinghouse owned and run by a woman named Mrs. Spriggs, who Mary referred to as a "most estimable lady." Her home was situated on land that is now the site of the Library of Congress. Mrs. Spriggs' boardinghouse was informally known as the Abolition House because many of the radical antislavery congressmen roomed there.

Lincoln was instantly popular with his fellow boarders at Abolition House, and with his new colleagues in Congress, who loved listening to his stories. During a meal, when something reminded Lincoln of a story, he would "lay down his knife and fork, place his elbows upon the table, rest his face between his hands, and begin with the words 'that reminds me . . .' and everybody prepared for the explosions that would follow."

While Lincoln's humor and storytelling kept him at the center of appreciative crowds, Mary was lonely and disappointed by life in Washington. Washington was the center of American politics with an exciting round of formal social events, but Mary was left all day and most evenings in the boardinghouse to care for her sons. Under the standards of the times, a woman could not attend formal parties or social gatherings without her husband—and Lincoln was too busy to take her. Moreover, Lincoln was not much interested in that sort of thing, preferring casual gatherings with friends where he could sit back, talk politics, and exchange stories. It was unthinkable to include a woman at such gatherings.

None of the other congressmen boarding at Abolition House had brought their families, so Mary was without company. One Washington resident observed that the town was not kind or welcoming to the members' wives. Mary's loneliness was exacerbated because her bold personality, her temper, and her unruly and poorly disciplined boys made her unpopular with the other boarders, who disapproved of her indulgent parenting.

In the spring, Mary and the boys left Washington. The

Lincolns never publicly stated her reasons, but Mary told her
sister that she feared that her presence was hindering Lincoln
in his work. She couldn't return to Springfield because they had
rented their house for two years. She went instead to stay at her
father's house in Kentucky.

✳   ✳   ✳   ✳   ✳   ✳   ✳   ✳   ✳   ✳   ✳   ✳   ✳   ✳   ✳

Slave pens and auction blocks were a common sight in
Washington, D.C., giving Lincoln his first sustained,
close-up look at the horrors of slavery. One day an incident
occurred with a black waiter at the boardinghouse where Lincoln
and a number of other congressmen ate their meals. The waiter
was working to buy his freedom for three hundred dollars. He
had earned two hundred forty dollars and needed only another
sixty when his master changed his mind and ordered the police to
take him into custody. The officers, "in the presence of his wife,
gagged him, placed him in irons, and, with loaded pistols, forced
him into one of the slave prisons."

Joshua Giddings, an antislavery representative from Ohio,
demanded an investigation into the brutality of the incident.
Former president John Quincy Adams—who decades earlier
had lost his bid for reelection to Andrew Jackson—was serving

as congressman from Massachusetts. Adams led the antislavery coalition that included Giddings and others. Previously they had tried to outlaw slavery in the lands acquired from Mexico, but failed. Now Adams, Giddings, Lincoln, and others introduced a bill outlawing slave trading in the nation's capital. Jackson's former vice president, John Calhoun, now serving as senator from South Carolina, and other proslavery congressmen blocked it.

Meanwhile in Kentucky, Lincoln's father-in-law, Robert Todd, and Henry Clay proposed a plan for gradually emancipating the slaves in the state. To the surprise of many, the voters of Kentucky—even those who did not own slaves—overwhelmingly voted against the plan. Lincoln felt discouraged by the flat refusal of so many white Southerners, even those who were not slave owners, to end slavery. A young Kentuckian explained to Lincoln that slave ownership was the highest possible status symbol— and nobody wanted to give it up. "You might have any amount of land; money in your pocket or bank stock and while traveling around, no body would be any wiser, but if you had a darkey trudging at your heels every body would see him and know you owned slaves." Lincoln understood such a prospect was "highly seductive to thoughtless and giddy headed young men."

★ ★ ★ ★ ★ ★ ★ ★ ★ ★ ★ ★ ★ ★ ★

Thomas Jefferson, a slave owner, struggled with the cruelty of slavery, saying, "there is nothing I would not sacrifice to a practicable plan of abolishing every vestige of this moral and political depravity."

During the decades after Jefferson's death, slavery became more and more deeply entrenched in the Southern way of life. Enslaved workers served in homes as butlers, housekeepers, and nannies. Plantations depended on slave labor. In the words of former vice president John Calhoun:

> We of the South will not, cannot, surrender our institutions. [Slavery] cannot be subverted without drenching the country in blood, and extirpating one or the other of the races.

Instead of seeing slavery as a necessary evil, like Thomas Jefferson, Calhoun insisted that slavery was a *positive good*, and was "indispensible for the happiness" of *both* races—a view based on the idea that blacks were inferior and fit only for slavery.

L incoln didn't believe he could change deeply entrenched attitudes toward slavery, and because Whigs were in the minority, he wasn't able to create any internal improvements, so he worked to strengthen the Whig Party. In an attempt to weaken the Democrats, he pounced when President Polk lied about the start of the Mexican War. When Polk falsely claimed that the Mexicans had been the aggressors, Lincoln made it clear that the spot where blood was first spilled was not on American soil.

The tactic backfired. Lincoln was called "Spotty Lincoln" and attacked by the newspapers for unpatriotically questioning the Mexican War.

After experiencing one failure after another, Lincoln grew discouraged. His letters to Mary made clear that he longed for his law practice, and he missed his family. "I hate to stay in this old room by myself," he wrote to Mary, "having nothing but business, no variety." He missed his sons, saying, "Don't let the blessed fellows forget father."

Lincoln did find one cause in which he could succeed. Eliza Hamilton and Dolley Madison, the aging widows of Founding Fathers Alexander Hamilton and James Madison, joined with Louisa Adams, wife of John Quincy Adams, to raise money to build the Washington Monument. Lincoln, who had admired George Washington since reading his biography as a young man, threw his support behind the proposed monument. He helped manage fundraising events. By July of 1848, the three widows had raised enough money to justify laying the cornerstone. At a ceremony held on July 4, 1848, Eliza Hamilton, Dolley Madison, Lincoln, and twenty thousand others gathered to watch as the Washington Monument cornerstone was put in place.

✶ ✶ ✶ ✶ ✶ ✶ ✶ ✶ ✶ ✶ ✶ ✶ ✶ ✶ ✶

At the conclusion of Lincoln's two-year term in Congress, he joined his family and they returned home to Springfield. Believing that his public career was over, Lincoln turned his back on politics and plunged into his law practice. Mary, however, never lost faith in her husband's public career. About this time she told a personal friend that Lincoln "is to be president of the United States someday; if I had not thought so, I would never have married him, for you can see he is not pretty."

Lincoln's legal practice continued growing as railroads and other industries moved into Illinois and sought out his services.

Laying corner stone, Washington Monument, by The Knapp Co., c. 1893

GEN. GEO. WASHINGTON.

LAYING CORNER STONE, WASHINGTON MONUMENT

While he was a master in the courtroom, he believed a lawyer best served his clients in the role of peacemaker, resorting to lawsuits only when absolutely necessary. Whenever a client wanted to sue over an unimportant matter or a trivial sum, Lincoln advised him to drop the matter as not worth the time or energy. One client persisted, saying he wanted to "show the blamed rascal up." Lincoln replied, offering a method of dealing with rascals that he took to his own heart. "My friend," he said, "if you are going into the business of showing up every rascal you meet, you will have no time to do anything else the rest of your life."

Reentering Politics

*If a man will stand up and assert, and repeat
and reassert, that two and two do not make four,
I know nothing in the power of argument
that can stop him.*

— Abraham Lincoln

n December of 1849, the Lincolns' youngest son, three-year-old Eddie, came down with tuberculosis, an illness with no known cure. He was sick for almost two months. On February 1, 1850, Eddie died. Neighbors heard Mary weeping inconsolably. For days she could not stop crying, would not get out of bed, and refused to eat. "Eat, Mary," Lincoln begged her, "for we must live." Lincoln, never expressive with his own emotions, simply said, "We miss him very much."

Later that same year, Lincoln received a letter from his

stepbrother, Johnston, telling him that his father was dying and was begging to see him. A cousin also wrote to say that Thomas Lincoln had experienced a seizure of the heart and was begging to see his only son. Lincoln believed relatives were exaggerating his father's illness. He and Mary were still in mourning for Eddie. To support the family, he was working long hours. His life became complicated when, within months of Eddie's death, Mary was once more expecting a child. Her pregnancy was a difficult one. Lincoln wrote back to Johnston, saying, "My business is such that I could hardly leave home now, if it were not, as it is that my own wife is sick-abed. It is a case of baby sickness, and I suppose it not dangerous. I sincerely hope Father may yet recover his health." He added, "Say to him that if we could meet now, it is doubtful whether it would not be more painful than pleasant."

The Lincolns' third son, William Wallace, was born on December 21, 1850. About a month later, Lincoln's father died. Lincoln didn't attend the funeral, which some historians interpret as callousness toward a father he never particularly liked, and evidence of a cold and detached nature. Others, though, suggest that it was just as likely that Lincoln simply couldn't go because of the difficulty of the journey, the birth of a child, and his load of legal work.

Two and a half years later, on April 4, 1853, when Lincoln's fourth and youngest son was born, he paid respect to his father by naming the child Thomas Lincoln. Baby Thomas's head was unusually large for his body, prompting Lincoln to joke that his son resembled a wiggly little tadpole. The family called the baby "Tad." The nickname stuck for the rest of Tad's life.

✶ ✶ ✶ ✶ ✶ ✶ ✶ ✶ ✶ ✶ ✶ ✶ ✶ ✶ ✶

Lincoln was roused from semiretirement from politics when both houses of Congress approved the Kansas-Nebraska Act, one of the bitterest and most divisive laws in American history. The act would overturn the Missouri Compromise and allow slavery to expand to *all* the new territories. Stephen Douglas, Mary's former admirer, now a U.S. senator from Illinois, was the one who had shepherded the Kansas-Nebraska Act through both houses of Congress. The bill became law on May 30, 1854 when signed by Democratic president Franklin Pierce.

Lincoln later said that when the law passed, he and the other Whigs in Illinois were "thunderstruck and stunned; and we reeled and fell in utter confusion." Lincoln received the news while he and a colleague, attorney T. Lyle Dickey, were practicing in an out-of-town court and rooming together. The night they learned

Political map of the United States showing the slave states, free states, and territories open to slavery by the repeal of the Missouri Compromise, by William Reynolds and J. C. Jones, 1856

that the bill passed, they sat up in their room and discussed the news far into the night. When morning came, Lincoln was still awake, deeply absorbed in thought. He turned and said, "I tell you, Dickey, this nation cannot exist half-slave and half-free."

Until then, Lincoln believed that eventually slavery would die out on its own. Now he knew better. With the Kansas-Nebraska Act in place, slave owners rushed to Kansas and Nebraska to vote in the first elections over slavery. Fraud in the first elections was blatant. In one precinct, legal residents cast only twenty ballots out of six hundred. The proslavery faction claimed power and immediately passed laws leveling harsh punishment against anyone who spoke out against slavery. They went so far as to establish a death penalty for anyone who helped runaway slaves.

Outraged abolitionists set up their own government in Topeka, Kansas. David Atchison, a proslavery Missouri senator, proclaimed the abolitionists to be "negro thieves" and "tyrants," and encouraged settlers to defend their "institution" with "the bayonet and with blood," and if necessary, "to kill every God-d—abolitionist in the district." So much fighting and killing broke out that Kansas was called "Bloody Kansas" and "Bleeding Kansas." After Massachusetts senator Charles Sumner criticized the Kansas-Nebraska act, a senator from South Carolina,

Unnamed "Border Ruffians," proslavery activists from Missouri who crossed the border into Kansas Territory to promote slavery. Photographed in Clinton, Iowa, by Blackall, between 1854 and 1860.

Preston Brooks, bludgeoned him at his desk and badly wounded him. President Pierce sent federal troops to stop the killing and violence. Pierce also instructed the federal troops to distribute proslavery literature.

✶ ✶ ✶ ✶ ✶ ✶ ✶ ✶ ✶ ✶ ✶ ✶ ✶ ✶ ✶

To defend the Kansas-Nebraska Act, Senator Douglas spoke for three hours at the annual fair in Springfield in front of a large crowd. He argued that the new law rested on the principle of self-government—the people themselves must decide whether or not to allow slavery in the territories. He called the principle "popular sovereignty." He argued that if Southerners were allowed to bring their hogs into Kansas, they should also be allowed to bring their slaves.

Lincoln wanted to debate with Douglas in public, but Douglas refused to allow Lincoln to share the stage with him. So Lincoln spoke to the crowds without Douglas present. On October 16,

Stephen Douglas, photographed between 1855 and 1865, photographer unknown

he gave his first antislavery speech to the largest audience he'd ever addressed. He began in a hesitant and halting manner. As he warmed to the subject of the evils of slavery, he grew more impassioned. He took his audience back to their roots as a people and the founding of the nation. He argued that self-government meant *all* people were created equal and entitled to control their own destinies. He said that government in which some oppressed others was not self-government. It was tyranny.

"Nearly eighty years ago," he said, "we began by declaring that all men are created equal; but now from that beginning we have run down to the other declaration, that for *some* men to enslave *others* is a 'sacred right of self-government.' These principles cannot stand together."

In response to Douglas's statement that if Southerners could take their hogs to Nebraska, they should also be allowed to take their slaves, Lincoln said it would be correct if there was no difference between hogs and men. That brought him to the heart of the issue, which was "whether the Negro is *not* or *is* a man." If the Negro was a man, he had a right to be included in "we the *people*." Douglas, Lincoln pointed out, "has no very vivid impression that the Negro is a human."

Lincoln's remarks were published in the newspapers. After

daring to suggest that blacks were human, Lincoln found himself awash in a sea of racism and hatred. Democratic newspapers called him and others opposed to the act "n— worshippers," and "n— agitators," and shameless thieves.

Lincoln's emotional detachment, which so frustrated his wife, allowed him to remain calm in a storm of furious name-calling. He gave talks, sprinkling his lawyerly arguments with stories to illustrate his points. While speaking in Bloomington, he said Douglas's popular sovereignty reminded him of a story:

A man went into a restaurant and called for a ginger cake, which was handed to him—but spying the sign 'Sweet Cider For Sale' he handed the cake back and said he would take a glass of cider in its place. After drinking the cider he got up to leave, whereupon the keeper called to him to pay for his cider.

The customer replied: 'Cider? Why I gave you the cake for the cider.'

'Well then pay me for the cake.'

'Pay you for the cake? I didn't have the cake.'

Whereupon the keeper scratched his head and said,
'Well,' that is so but it seems to me I am cheated some way.'

Lincoln concluded the story by remarking that someone was bound to be cheated by Mr. Douglas's theory of popular sovereignty.

Lincoln was particularly annoyed by the portion of the Kansas-Nebraska Act that said the true intent of the act was not to allow or prevent slavery in any state or territory, but instead to "leave the people free to form and regulate their domestic institutions in their own way." So he wrote an editorial that included a story:

Abraham Lincoln has a fine meadow containing a beautiful spring of water. His neighbor, John Calhoun, becomes the owner of a large herd of cattle. Calhoun, casting a longing eye on Lincoln's meadow, dismantles Lincoln's fence.

"You rascal," says Lincoln. "What have you done?"

"Oh," replies Calhoun, "everything is right. I have taken down your fence; but nothing more. It is my true intent and meaning not to drive my cattle into your meadow, nor to exclude them from your meadow, but to leave them perfectly free to form their own notions of the food and to direct their movement in their own way!"

Lincoln read the proslavery newspapers and wrote memoranda to himself laying out the counterarguments. He didn't try to talk people out of their deeply rooted racial prejudices. Instead he focused entirely on logic. "If A. can prove, however conclusively, that he may, of right, enslave B," Lincoln wrote, "why may not B. snatch the same argument and prove equally, that he may enslave A?" In response to the argument that whites were justified in enslaving blacks on the grounds of race, he wrote, "By this rule, you are to be slave to the first man you meet with a fairer skin than your own." In response to those who argued that blacks were less intelligent and therefore fit only for slavery, he wrote, "By this rule, you are to be slave to the first man you meet with an intellect superior to your own."

Indeed, some newspapers were arguing precisely that. The *Charleston Mercury* suggested that just as enslaving blacks was a positive good for society, enslaving poor and uneducated laboring whites would also benefit everyone. "Make the laboring man the slave of one man," declared George Fitzhugh of Virginia, "instead of the slave of society, and he would be far better off." The *Charleston Mercury* stated that "slavery is the natural and normal condition of the laboring man, whether white or black." Another newspaper, the *New York Day-Book* also endorsed the idea of enslaving laboring whites. At the same time, growing numbers of white laborers in the North opposed slavery. There arose a Northern antislavery party and anti-immigration party called the American Party, also known as the Know-Nothings because they started as a secret order, and when asked about their party affiliation, said they knew nothing.

Until 1840, Protestantism was the dominant religion in America. Around 1840 the first large waves of Catholic immigrants came to America. The Know-Nothings wanted to restrict immigration. American Party members viewed Catholic immigrants as strange, foreign, less American, and in many cases, less

A Know-Nothing party anti-Catholic cartoon stoking fears about immigrants

white. The Party slogan was that "Americans shall rule America," where "Americans" were understood to be people of northern European ancestry. They also called themselves the "Nativists" and "Native Americans" on the idea that white Protestant settlers were the first and true Americans.

Knowing that Lincoln, too, was antislavery, the American Party asked Lincoln to run as one of their candidates. Lincoln refused. At the same time, he was unable to resist pointing out the irony of the Know-Nothings calling themselves Nativists. "Do not the [Native Americans] wear breechcloth and carry tomahawks?" he asked. "We pushed them from their homes, and now turn upon others not fortunate enough to come over as early as we or our forefathers."

Meanwhile, another radical movement was stirring in the United States: The women's movement, headed by Elizabeth Cady Stanton, Lucretia Mott, Susan B. Anthony, and Sojourner Truth. The women's movement wanted rights for women—including the right to vote and own property. Very few people in the country took the women's rights advocates seriously. During the early years of the movement, they were the subjects of widespread mockery.

The women's activists were also abolitionists, working closely with such leaders as Frederick Douglass, a former slave

Frederick Douglass, by John White
Hurn, 1862

and brilliant speaker. Douglass attended the very first women's convention held in 1848 in Seneca Falls, New York.

The abolitionists and women's rights groups understood that they were fighting the same enemy: the concept of paternalism.

★ ★ ★ ★ ★ ★ ★ ★ ★ ★ ★ ★ ★ ★ ★

Diving back into politics, Lincoln set his sights on winning the 1855 Whig nomination for U.S. senator. He was "warmly encouraged in his aspirations by his wife." He was quietly gathering support among his friends and Whig Party insiders when his campaign was almost derailed: Without his knowledge or consent, someone nominated him for the state Assembly, which would have made it impossible to run for the Senate, because at that time the state assemblymen selected the U.S. senators.

Mary was the one who marched to the newspaper office and demanded that his name be removed. She imperiously stated that her husband was destined for greater things. William Jayne, a local politician and physician, called on Lincoln at home and asked if he would allow his name to be reinstated. Lincoln

Paternalism, deeply entrenched in the South and elsewhere, held that there was a natural hierarchy in society with white men at the top and black women at the bottom. Under the doctrine of paternalism, white men were considered naturally superior. Inferiors—including blacks, women, and Native Americans—were viewed like children. In the paternalistic worldview, white men, taking on the role of a parent, must care for inferiors, provide for them—and punish them when they misbehave. Corporal punishment at the time was widely accepted, justified by the Biblical verse, "Spare the rod, spoil the child," so beating slaves, children—and even wives—was socially acceptable and legal. A cornerstone of paternalism was the belief that white women and all people of color were better off under the dominion of white men.

refused, implying that he had no choice but to give in to Mary's pleading that he run for the Senate instead.

Lincoln campaigned for the Senate by writing letters to supporters throughout the state. As Election Day approached, he was feeling cautiously optimistic. After the first round of voting, he had forty-five votes, the Democratic nominee had forty-one, and Lyman Trumbull, a Democrat who opposed the Kansas-Nebraska Act, had five. Because nobody received a majority, the voting had to be repeated until one candidate reached a majority. By the eighth ballot, enough Democrats switched their vote to Trumbull to make it clear that he would emerge the winner.

Lincoln was deeply frustrated that his forty-five supporters had to yield to Trumbull's five. In private, he sank into a depression, but he hid his disappointment in public and maintained his warm friendship with Trumbull. His consolation was that even though he lost, he'd started with the most votes, and the decision had been made by a handful of legislators and not the voters themselves.

The Birth of the Republican Party

Repeal the Missouri Compromise—repeal all compromises—
repeal the Declaration of Independence—repeal all past history,
you still cannot repeal human nature. It will be the abundance
of man's heart that slavery extension is wrong; and out of
the abundance of his heart, his mouth will continue to speak.

— Abraham Lincoln

y 1855 it was clear to those who wanted to stop the spread of slavery that a new political party was necessary. The Whigs, divided over the issue of slavery, were no longer a viable party. The abolitionists were viewed as too extreme and radical to gain widespread popular support. The Know-Nothings had too many enemies.

A new party started in Ripon, Wisconsin, when former members of the Whig Party met to oppose the spread of slavery into the territories. The group called themselves the Republicans and rapidly gained members throughout the North and West. The Republican Party in Illinois got started when Paul Selby, editor of the Jacksonville *Morgan Journal* suggested a conference for newspaper editors opposed to the Kansas-Nebraska Act. They invited Lincoln to attend. When the group met in Decatur on February 22, 1856, Lincoln was the only attendee who was not a journalist.

Lincoln helped write the new party's platform. The first

While the Democrats and Republicans are still the two major parties in the United States today, the Republican and Democratic parties of the twenty-first century have very little in common with those of the nineteenth century. During Lincoln's time, the Democrats were the party of the South and the Confederacy.

During the first part of the twentieth century, the Democrats supported the Ku Klux Klan, white supremacy, and Jim Crow laws. After Democratic president Franklin D. Roosevelt expanded the federal government through major spending programs, and Democrats John F. Kennedy and Lyndon B. Johnson supported the Civil

plank called for overturning the Kansas-Nebraska Act. To attract Democrats opposed to the Kansas-Nebraska Act, they called for restoring the Missouri Compromise and acknowledging that slavery and the Fugitive Slave Law were supported by the Constitution. To attract the more radical abolitionists, they agreed that the United States was founded on the concept of freedom, and that slavery—while allowed by the Constitution—was wrong. They made themselves welcome to those who were foreign born

Rights Act, guaranteeing certain rights to minorities and people of color, there was a great shift in the parties. The Democratic Party became the party of civil rights, government programs and regulations, and urban and minority communities. The Democrats who were annoyed by these changes gradually drifted to the Republican Party. The Republican Party facilitated the shift by appealing to those who wanted to follow Thomas Jefferson's notions of the sanctity of states' rights. As a result, the Republican Party came to draw much of its strength from rural, white America—the very people who had once been ardent Democrats.

and Catholic. To attract Henry Clay Whigs, they declared themselves the party of scientific progress and federal programs.

When the Illinois Republicans met on May 29 to officially announce the state's new party, Lincoln offered the final words. He took the stage and gave what was, by all accounts, an electrifying speech. No written record of the speech exists, so it has come to be called Lincoln's Lost Speech. Snippets were recorded by journalists. Lincoln talked about the evils of slavery and stirred pity by talking about "the music of an overseer's lash upon a mulatto girl's back." Nathaniel Niles, editor of *The Belleville Advocate*, wrote: "Abraham Lincoln, by his wonderful eloquence electrified the audience of two thousand men." Another witness said, "For an hour and a half he held the assemblage spell-bound . . . When he concluded, the audience sprang to their feet, and cheer after cheer told how deeply their hearts had been touched, and their souls warmed."

✷ ✷ ✷ ✷ ✷ ✷ ✷ ✷ ✷ ✷ ✷ ✷ ✷ ✷

On March 6, 1857, the United States Supreme Court sent shockwaves rippling through the North and relief throughout the South with its decision in a case called *Dred Scott v. Sandford.*

The Birth of the Republican Party

Dred Scott was an enslaved man whose master, a surgeon in the U.S. Army, took him out of Missouri into the free state of Illinois, then into the free territory of Wisconsin. Dred Scott sued for his freedom based on the fact that he was then living in a free state. In 1847 the case went to court in Missouri, where the law could be summarized as "once free, always free," intended to prevent free blacks from being kidnapped and sold into bondage. A lower Missouri court ruled for Dred Scott, declaring him a free man. His former master appealed. After ten years of appeals and reversals and retrials, the case went all the way to the U.S. Supreme Court.

The issue before the court was straightforward: Was Dred Scott free? Reaching an answer required wading into the highly political question of whether Southerners could bring their slaves into free states and territories. The Supreme Court was stacked against Dred Scott. A majority of the justices were staunchly proslavery, and the chief justice, Roger B. Taney,

Dred Scott, published by Century Company, 1887

had been a close friend of Andrew Jackson, and a member of Jackson's "Kitchen Cabinet" of trusted advisers.

Roger Taney, writing for the Supreme Court, ruled against Dred Scott, holding that he remained a slave even after being brought into Illinois and Wisconsin. The court justified its ruling by stating that blacks "had for more than a century before been regarded as beings of an inferior order, and altogether unfit to associate with the white race either in social or political relations, and so far inferior that they had no rights which the white man was bound to respect, and might justly and lawfully be reduced to slavery for his benefit." The court also declared that no person of African descent, whether free or slave, could *ever* be a citizen of the United States. According to the Court the phrase "We the People" did not include—and was not intended to include, and moreover could *never* include—those descended from African races.

Roger B. Taney, chief justice of the United States, 1836–1864, photographed between 1855 and 1865, photographer unknown

The court then went on to say that the federal government

had no constitutional right to restrict slavery *anywhere*, and thus the Missouri Compromise was unconstitutional. In declaring the Missouri Compromise unconstitutional, the Supreme Court undercut the entire platform of the new Republican Party. Taney's goal was to end the controversial slavery question once and for all by deciding for the proslavery side and for the South— the side he believed was right.

Once the Supreme Court interprets the Constitution, there are two ways to alter the court's ruling. The Supreme Court can decide to *overrule* itself, which rarely happens. The American court system is based on the idea of *precedent*: To create stability, court decisions become rules that later courts must follow. If courts constantly overturn their own rules, there would be a lack of stability and nobody would know what was legal and what was not.

The only other way to overturn the Supreme Court's interpretation of the Constitution is through the cumbersome process of amending the Constitution.

Instead of ending the controversy, as Taney intended, *Dred Scott v. Sandford* roused the Republicans to fight harder. Some Northerners called for the court's decision to be ignored. Lincoln, who never advocated ignoring laws or rulings, said simply that the Supreme Court had overruled itself in the past and must be persuaded to do so again. He didn't explain how. With seven proslavery justices on the court, an equal balance of slave states and free states, and deeply entrenched racism throughout the North, overturning the decision seemed impossible.

Senator Douglas returned from Washington, D.C. to give speeches in support of the Supreme Court's ruling. Lincoln, as had become his habit, gave speeches responding to each of Douglas's points, explaining why both Douglas and the court were wrong.

✶ ✶ ✶ ✶ ✶ ✶ ✶ ✶ ✶ ✶ ✶ ✶ ✶ ✶ ✶

Lincoln, still busy with his law practice, traveled with his family to New York in July of 1857 to collect a large fee due to him from one of his corporate clients. He and Mary did some sightseeing in New York, and then traveled to Niagara and Canada. Lincoln's strongest memory of the trip was how the grand falls inspired him to meditate on the indefinite past—the

The Birth of the Republican Party

continent as it existed before Columbus and at the time of the
ancient mammals that roamed the land. Mary, on the other hand,
recalled seeing the steamers in New York's harbor and longing to
live the life of a wealthy woman and visit Europe. She jokingly
told Lincoln that her next husband would be rich.

Mary encouraged Lincoln to throw himself back into politics. After they returned home, he began working to organize the
Republicans with the hope of taking Douglas's Senate seat in the
coming 1858 election. He and his fellow Republicans drew up
lists of voters by precincts, paying personal visits to sympathetic
voters, stressing the importance of electing Republicans to the
Senate. Lincoln's own supporters, who included his law partner
Herndon, persuaded enough Republican leaders to back Lincoln as the nominee for Senator that when the Republican Party
of Illinois met on June 16, 1858, support for Lincoln was over-
whelming. The Chicago delegation unfurled a banner proclaiming
"Cook County is for Abraham Lincoln" to enthusiastic cheers.
Someone made a motion to change the banner to "Illinois is for
Abraham Lincoln," and a thunderous applause filled the hall.

Abraham Lincoln was unanimously named the Republican
nominee for Senator. He took great care with his acceptance
speech. Friends who had read drafts advised him to tone it down,

113

warning that his position was too extreme. He asked, "Isn't it true?" His friend and confidant, Samuel C. Parks, responded with, "Certainly it is true, but it is premature. The people are not prepared for it, and Douglas will beat us with it all over the state." Lincoln replied, "I think that the time has come to say it, and will let it go as it is."

That evening, addressing a packed hall, Lincoln delivered the speech that became one of his most famous:

> *A house divided against itself cannot stand. I believe this government cannot endure, permanently, half slave and half free. I do not expect the Union to be dissolved—I do not expect the house to fall—but I do expect it will cease to be divided. It will become all one thing or all the other. Either the opponents of slavery will arrest the further spread of it, and place it where the public mind shall rest in the belief that it is in the course of ultimate extinction; or its advocates will push it forward, till it shall become lawful in all the States, old as well as new—North as well as South.*

He pointed out how the Supreme Court's decision in *Dred Scott* easily opened the door to Illinois—and all Northern states—to become slave states: If masters could bring their slaves into the free states, and the slaves remained enslaved, what prevented them from bringing *thousands* of slaves into the free states? Lincoln argued that it was a simple step from *Dred Scott* to a law stating that no state could forbid slavery.

Lincoln and Stephen Douglas were now locked in a battle to be the Senator from Illinois. With the campaign under way, Lincoln challenged Douglas to a series of debates. Even though the winner would be selected by the legislature, Lincoln wanted to bring his arguments directly to the people. This time Douglas agreed.

The first debate between Lincoln and Douglas took place in Ottawa before a record-breaking crowd of more than ten thousand. People flocked to Ottawa on horseback, on hayracks, and on foot. Special trains were chartered to bring citizens from Chicago, Peru, and LaSalle. On the stage, Lincoln and Douglas sparred and disagreed— with Douglas defending slavery and Lincoln attacking it. Because newspapers published their speeches and arguments far and wide, Lincoln had his first truly national exposure.

Lincoln-Douglas Debates Commemorative Stamp, by U.S. Post Office Department, 1958

Over the next few months, Lincoln and Douglas engaged in six more debates held throughout Illinois, one in each of the congressional districts. During the course of these debates, Lincoln made many statements in which he seemed to waver on the issue of racial equality. His enemies accused him of being deliberately vague.

For example, while defending himself against the charge that he was in favor of the intermarrying and social equality between the races, Lincoln insisted that he'd never claimed that there was perfect social and political equality between the races. He then went on to present his position:

> *I will say here, while upon this subject, that I have no purpose, directly or indirectly, to interfere with the institution of slavery in the States where it exists. I believe I have no lawful right to do so, and I have no inclination to do so.*

The proslavery side heard hedging and hairsplitting. Instead of arguing that slavery was a positive benefit for society, he was simply saying that he had no legal right to abolish slavery—which to the proslavery side was nothing more than a factual statement. They were annoyed that he refused to guarantee the right to own slaves. The abolitionists were even less pleased with his comments.

He went on to say:

I have no purpose to introduce political and social equality between the white and black races. There is a physical difference between the two, which, in my judgment, will probably forever forbid their living together upon the footing of perfect equality, and inasmuch as it becomes a necessity that there must be a difference, I, as well as Judge Douglas, am in favor of the race to which I belong having the superior position. I have never said anything to the contrary.

At first glance, he seemed to be saying that whites were superior. Upon closer inspection, though, he pointed out only a *physical* difference between the races. He then said, "inasmuch as it becomes a necessity that there must be a difference," he preferred for the race to which he belonged to be named the superior one. The comment could have been understood as a lawyerly hypothetical: If the difference in color means the races cannot be equal, Lincoln—like Douglas—preferred for his race to be named the superior one. It was a lawyerly dodge over whether blacks were naturally inferior.

In another speech, he said:

I have said that I do not understand the Declaration to mean that all men were created equal in all respects.

Certainly the Negro is not our equal in color—perhaps not in many other respects; still, in the right to put into his mouth the bread that his own hands have earned, he is the equal of every other man. In pointing out that more has been given to you, you cannot be justified in taking away the little which has been given to him. If God gave him but little, that little let him enjoy.

Lincoln's defenders point out that all he really did in the above speech was admit that there was inequality, or difference, in skin color. He never actually said blacks were inferior—he merely admitted the possibility. The thrust of the argument was another lawyerly hypothetical: Even if the blacks *were* inferior, that would not warrant taking away their rights.

The abolitionists demanded to know why he didn't just come out and say that the races were equal and slavery was morally wrong. Why all this hairsplitting and runaround talk? Lincoln's critics accused him of kicking up dust so nobody could figure out exactly where he stood.

While Lincoln annoyed both sides, he managed to position himself as a moderate who walked the middle and avoided extremes. It isn't clear whether he really *was* a moderate, or whether he understood that the only way to get elected was to come across as a moderate.

✯ ✯ ✯ ✯ ✯ ✯ ✯ ✯ ✯ ✯ ✯ ✯ ✯ ✯ ✯

Both Lincoln and Mary were pessimistic about his chances. Mary was dispirited as Election Day approached, and even a family friend assuring her that Lincoln had a good chance at winning the senate seat didn't cheer her up.

Indeed, on January 5, 1859, the legislature elected Douglas fifty-four to forty-six. For the second time, Lincoln was defeated in his bid to become a senator. That evening his friend Henry C. Whitney found him alone in his office "gloomy as midnight." According to Whitney, Lincoln was "completely steeped in the bitter waters of hopelessness and despair said several times with bitterness, 'I expect everybody to desert me.'"

Later Lincoln came to see his defeat as a mere bump in the road. Some friends told him he lost the election because his position was too radical for the majority of voters and because his "House Divided" speech had alarmed too many people. "Well Gentlemen," Lincoln replied, "you may think that speech was a mistake, but I never have believed it was, and you will see the day when you will consider it was the wisest thing I ever said."

President Lincoln

he very next year, 1860, was the year of a presidential election. Immediately after Lincoln lost the race for the Senate, his supporters and various Illinois newspapers floated the idea of Lincoln for president. He always laughed off the notion. "Mary insists," he told a reporter, "that I am going to be Senator and President of the United States." Then, "shaking all over with mirth at his wife's ambition," he exclaimed, "'Just think of such a sucker as me as President.'"

It *was* a bit preposterous. He'd spent a single term as a

congressman without distinction. Twice he'd lost his attempt to become a senator. His only national fame came from his public debates with Douglas. He had no organized support outside of Illinois. He had limited governing experience. But he admitted to friends that, "The taste is in my mouth a little."

In April of 1860, he went on a speaking tour to the East Coast, where he also visited his son Robert, who was attending Phillips Exeter preparatory school in New Hampshire. After drawing large and appreciative audiences, he authorized a group of friends and supporters to quietly lay the groundwork for a presidential campaign. What gave him hope was that, although there would be serious competition for the Republican nomination, each of his competitors was a flawed candidate. William Seward, New York senator and former governor, was widely considered the leading candidate for the nomination. He was experienced and well liked and one of the original founders of the national Republican Party—but he had a reputation for being an extremist and abolitionist, which could harm his chances of obtaining a majority of votes. Salmon Chase, governor of Ohio, was a popular antislavery activist and considered less radical, but he lacked personal magnetism and was an ineffective speaker. Edward Bates, a former Whig, had very little popular backing and had never even joined the Republican Party.

Even though Lincoln was less well known and less experienced than Seward, Chase, or Bates, some Republican leaders saw him as more electable because he was more moderate. Moreover, because he had never held a major office, he had fewer enemies. He had never held power, so he'd had fewer chances to make the sort of blunders and missteps that haunt presidential candidates.

Lincoln knew he could never muster more support than Seward. His strategy was to slow Seward's momentum while trying to be the second choice of a large enough number of delegates so that if none of the others achieved a majority after the first ballot, he might accumulate votes as others dropped out. He didn't want to get too far ahead too soon lest the leading candidates turn their attention to stopping him instead of attacking one other.

William Seward,
by Julian Vannerson,
1859

Salmon Chase,
photographed between
1855 and 1865,
photographer unknown

Edward Bates,
photographed between
1855 and 1865,
photographer unknown

Lincoln's supporters successfully maneuvered to have the Republican National Convention held in Chicago, where Lincoln would have home advantage. The Republican convention opened in Chicago on May 16, 1860. Lincoln remained in Springfield, closely following events via telegram. Seward was so widely expected to win that a celebration crew was positioned outside his house in New York, ready to fire off a cannon salute when the word came of his victory. Some of Lincoln's key organizers were so sure Lincoln had no chance that they never arranged for a place to stay in Chicago.

On May 18, 1860, the day ballots were to be cast, Lincoln spent the morning playing a game of handball in a vacant lot with some friends, walking often to the telegraph office to get news of the voting. Soon came the word that after the first ballot, Seward had 173.5 votes, Lincoln 102, Chase 49, and Bates, 48. A candidate needed 233 to win. Lincoln's strong showing was the result of surprise defections from other candidates.

The telegram bearing the results of the second ballot showed that Seward had risen to 184.5 votes and Lincoln to 181. Lincoln knew then that he would win. Chase had fallen to 42.5, which meant he would soon drop out, freeing up his delegates. Because of Chase's longstanding rivalry with Seward, Lincoln knew that most of Chase's delegates would flock to him.

By the time the telegram bearing the results of the third ballot arrived in Springfield, a large crowd, rippling with excitement, gathered with Lincoln to await the results. Upon receiving word that he had secured the Republican nomination for president, Lincoln calmly accepted congratulations. Then he said, "I must go home. There is a little short woman there who is more interested in this matter than I am."

★ ★ ★ ★ ★ ★ ★ ★ ★ ★ ★ ★ ★ ★

Vice presidents at the time were selected by the nominating conventions. The Republicans nominated Hannibal Hamlin, a former senator and governor from Maine, as Lincoln's vice presidential running mate.

As the campaign got under way, Lincoln had to spend most of his time defending himself from false accusations. Democrats accused him of not believing in God. They accused him of slandering the name of Thomas Jefferson, attending Know-Nothing conventions, and failing to vote for supplies to the army during the Mexican War. He understood the Democrats hoped to goad him into refuting these charges, but he was unusually thick-skinned and not the type who *could* be goaded. His strategy was to pretend he wasn't paying attention, while quietly refuting the charges by publishing personal letters in newspapers showing the accusations false.

He positioned himself as humble, homespun Abraham Lincoln, the rail splitter—downplaying his position as an important and powerful lawyer representing the interests of the largest industries in Illinois. His supporters spread stories of his beginnings on a poor Kentucky farm and his honesty as a storekeeper.

Lincoln's road to the White House was made easier when the Democratic Party split into two factions, with the Northern Democrats favoring popular sovereignty while the Southern Democrats insisted that slaveholders should have the unfettered right to bring their "property" wherever they chose. At the Democratic convention held on June 18, 1860, anger boiled over. Lincoln's longtime rival, Stephen Douglas, won the Democratic nomination for president on a platform of popular sovereignty. When many Southerners did not get their wish of an even more proslavery platform, more than one hundred delegates walked out of the convention. They formed a new party, the National Democratic Party, and nominated their own candidate, John C. Breckinridge, who ran on a position that any restriction on slavery was unconstitutional.

Many Southern Cotton Whigs were opposed to slavery

expanding into the territories, but could not align themselves with the antislavery Republicans. They formed a party of their own, the Constitutional Union Party, and nominated their own candidate, former Tennessee senator John Bell.

With the proslavery vote divided between three candidates, Lincoln knew that to win the presidency he needed only to win over his Republican rivals for the nomination. He immediately began reaching out to his former rivals and their supporters.

★ ★ ★ ★ ★ ★ ★ ★ ★ ★ ★ ★ ★ ★

Mary was apprehensive as Election Day approached. "I scarcely know how I would bear up under defeat," she said. Her husband remained calmer and less anxious. At about seven o'clock on Election Day, a nervous Mary remained at home while Lincoln went to the statehouse in Springfield where an exuberant crowd awaited him. He lingered for a while, and then went with some friends to the telegraph office to await the returns. Good news started rolling in. Lincoln won one key precinct after another. Virginia went for the Constitutional Union Party candidate, denying the Democrats an important Southern state. When Seward's stronghold, New York, went for Lincoln, the outcome was clear. "Springfield went off like one immense cannon report, with shouting from houses, shouting from stores, shouting from housetops, shouting everywhere."

When the final votes were tallied, Lincoln had 1,866,452 votes, Douglas 1,376,957, Breckinridge, 849,781, and Bell 588,879. Abraham Lincoln became the sixteenth president of the United States and the first president born west of the Appalachians. He had won with less than 40 percent of the popular vote and without a single electoral vote from the South.

The morning after the election, Lincoln visited the governor's suite at the statehouse and found it thronged with friends, reporters, and well-wishers. A farmer greeted Lincoln, saying, "Uncle Abe, I didn't vote for yer, but I am mighty glad yer elected just the same." Lincoln replied, "Well, my old friend, when a man has been tried and pronounced not guilty he hasn't any right to find fault with the jury."

✳ ✳ ✳ ✳ ✳ ✳ ✳ ✳ ✳ ✳ ✳ ✳ ✳ ✳ ✳

Mary Todd Lincoln got her childhood wish. In March, at Lincoln's inauguration, she would become the wife of the president of the United States.

Lincoln's closest friends, all of whom disapproved of Mary, agreed in this: Lincoln, while extraordinarily talented and intelligent, tended to sink into melancholy and needed to be prodded—and Mary did the prodding. Long before others saw Lincoln's potential, Mary knew what he was capable of. Whether she generously gave her husband the confidence he needed, or whether, as many of Lincoln's friends believed, she mercilessly nagged him into becoming president, her contemporaries agreed that without Mary there would never have been a President Abraham Lincoln.

A House Divided

*A majority held in restraint by constitutional checks
and limitations, and always changing easily with deliberate
changes of popular opinions and sentiments,
is the only true sovereign of a free people.*

— Abraham Lincoln

our days after Abraham Lincoln was elected president
of the United States, South Carolina called for a state-
wide convention to consider seceding from the United
States. Within the month, Mississippi, Florida, Alabama, Georgia, Louisiana, and Texas followed. Eventually they would be joined by North Carolina, Arkansas, Virginia,
and Tennessee, forming the Confederate States of America.

South Carolina moved swiftly. On December 20, 1860, South
Carolina declared itself no longer part of the United States, and

ordered the U.S. Army to abandon its forts and military bases within South Carolina's borders. Kentucky-born Robert Anderson, major in the U.S. Army and commanding officer in South Carolina, refused. He moved his men to the most secure fortress in the area, Fort Sumter, strategically placed at the entrance to the Charleston Harbor.

The North was divided on how to respond. Some wanted to let the South go. Others opposed any concessions at all to the South. Still others floated compromises that would keep the South in the Union. The problem for Lincoln was that the only compromises that had any chance of success with South Carolina included guaranteeing the South the right to bring their slaves into the territories.

The Constitution was silent on the issue of secession. When the states ratified the Constitution in 1789, did they enter a contract from which they could withdraw anytime? Or in signing, did they give up the right to secede? Fortunately for Lincoln, President Jackson—beloved figurehead of the Democratic Party and the South—paved the way for the idea that secession was illegal. While Jackson was president, South Carolina threatened to rebel over taxes it didn't like. Jackson avoided war with South Carolina, but made it clear that in his view, states did not have the right to secede or ignore federal laws.

Outgoing President Buchanan, a Democrat from Pennsylvania, was morally opposed to slavery and declared secession illegal, but he did nothing to stop the South. By February, the Confederate States of America had a working government, including temporary appointment of Jefferson Davis as president until elections could be arranged.

As Southern states seceded from the Union, many Southern senators and representatives abandoned their seats in Congress. Others were forced out for disloyalty or for taking up arms against the federal government. With the South and the Democratic Party underrepresented in Congress, the Republicans suddenly had a majority in both houses.

As the United States careened toward its greatest constitutional crisis, Lincoln prepared for his inauguration and put together his new administration. Instead of giving cabinet posts to his friends and colleagues from Illinois—the people he knew well and trusted—he appointed his rivals for the nomination, men he hardly knew, and men who remained outspoken in their opinion that Lincoln was inexperienced and not ready to lead. He cajoled a reluctant Seward to become his secretary of state. Mary didn't like Seward and she didn't want him appointed. She feared that Seward would get credit for any of Lincoln's accomplishments while Lincoln would take the blame for Seward's shortcomings. By seeking to influence Lincoln's choices, she earned criticism from observers. Women were not supposed to meddle in politics, which was seen exclusively as men's work. One observer said derisively that Mary tried to make herself into a sort of assistant president. Lincoln ignored her advice.

He also persuaded Seward's rival, Salmon Chase, to accept the post of secretary of the treasury. In doing so, he made sure that his cabinet represented a variety of viewpoints. It was a cabinet that could never be harmonious, but it was a cabinet that would force him to objectively examine all sides of all issues.

The Cabinet at Washington (Montgomery Blair, Caleb Smith, Salmon Chase, Abraham Lincoln, William Seward, Simon Cameron, Edward Bates, Gideon Welles). First published in *Harper's Weekly*, July 13, 1861.

✴ ✴ ✴ ✴ ✴ ✴ ✴ ✴ ✴ ✴ ✴ ✴ ✴ ✴ ✴

O n March 4, 1861, the day of Lincoln's inauguration, crowds gathered early. By the time the ceremony was about to begin, twenty-five thousand people stood in front of the Capitol building. Rumors were afloat of rebel plots to assassinate Lincoln or kidnap him before he could assume power, so two thousand volunteer soldiers stood guard. Sharpshooters were positioned on the roofs of the tallest buildings.

As was customary, the incoming president rode to his inauguration ceremony in an open carriage with the outgoing president. When Lincoln and Buchanan arrived at the East Portico of the Capitol Building, Edward Baker, now a U.S. senator, introduced Lincoln to the crowd. Lincoln took the stage and gave his inaugural address, which was filled with his usual poetry and flair, and included a plea to the South:

We must not be enemies. Though passion may have strained, it must not break our bonds of affection. The mystic chords of memory, stretching from every battlefield and patriot grave to every living heart and hearthstone all over this broad land, will yet swell the chorus of the Union, when again touched, as surely they will be, by the better angels of our nature.

Supreme Court Justice Roger Taney, author of the *Dred Scott* decision, administered the oath of office. Lincoln placed his hand on the Bible and solemnly swore to "preserve, protect and defend the Constitution of the United States." At the conclusion of the ceremony, Lincoln kissed the Bible, and "the crowd tossed hats into the air, wiped their eyes, and shouted till they grew hoarse."

✳ ✳ ✳ ✳ ✳ ✳ ✳ ✳ ✳ ✳ ✳ ✳ ✳ ✳ ✳

The first decision the new president had to make was a momentous one: Should he surrender Fort Sumter to South Carolina or send reinforcements to hold the fort? Surrendering would empower the South and was arguably an act of treason against the United States. On the other hand, sending reinforcements put the nation on the road to war. Lincoln's administration was divided. One of his generals, Winfield Scott, a Virginian and former Whig candidate for president, urged Lincoln to surrender Fort Sumter as the only way to retain the loyalty of Virginia.

Lincoln appeared unable to make a decision. Weeks dragged by. Lincoln thought so long and so deeply that his friends feared

The Inaugural Procession at Washington Passing the Gate of the Capitol Grounds, showing president-elect Lincoln and outgoing president Buchanan tipping his hat to the cheering crowd. Published in *Harper's Weekly*, March 16, 1861.

The Lincoln Family in 1861, picturing Mary Todd Lincoln, Willie, Robert, Tad, and the president, painted by F. B. Carpenter and engraved by J. C. Buttre, 1861

he'd sunk into another bout of melancholy. Then he made up his mind: He had taken an oath to defend the U.S. Constitution, which he understood to mean defending the Union created by that Constitution. Moreover, he believed South Carolina would accept nothing short of slavery expanding into the territories. He therefore ordered reinforcements sent to Major Anderson at Fort Sumter.

While bold action was contrary to Lincoln's deliberate and inward personality, once he made up his mind, he was difficult to budge. As Mary said of her husband, "when he set his foot down—none of us—no man nor woman could rule him after he had made up his mind." He now put his foot down firmly.

South Carolina must not be allowed to bully the United States.

On April 12, 1861, with the reinforcements still en route to Fort Sumter, Confederate artillery open fired on the fort. The Civil War had begun.

Bombardment of Fort Sumter, Charleston Harbor, 12th & 13th of April 1861, Currier & Ives, circa 1861

For two days, Major Anderson and his troops at Fort Sumter held out against the Confederate attack. Then on April 14, Anderson surrendered. The Confederacy cheered its first victory. On April 15, Lincoln called for seventy-five thousand militia volunteers—the first of many actions for which he would be accused of overstepping the limits on his power. The Constitution assigns to

Congress, not the president, the power to raise an army, but the new Congress was not yet in session. The Constitution also designates the president as commander in chief of the U.S. Armed Forces. Lincoln's justification for his action was that his role as commander in chief gave him powers over the military, and hence emergency war powers.

Free blacks responded to the call. They rushed to fight, but

The states that seceded from the Union and formed the Confederate States of America were those farthest south where the economy was completely dependent on slave labor. The eleven Confederate States were South Carolina, Mississippi, Florida, Alabama, Georgia, Louisiana, Texas, Arkansas, Virginia, Tennessee, and North Carolina.

The border states—Missouri, Delaware, Maryland, Kentucky, and West Virginia—were slave states, but a variety of factors kept slavery from becoming as deeply rooted there as in the Deep South. Cotton—the crop most suitable to slave labor—was not the dominant crop in the border states. Proximity to free states, which made

were turned away because of a 1792 law barring blacks from bearing arms for the U.S. Army. Immediately, abolitionist leader Frederick Douglass pushed for blacks to be allowed to serve as soldiers. "Once let the black man get upon his person the brass letter, U.S.," he famously said, "let him get an eagle on his button, and a musket on his shoulder and bullets in his pocket, there is no power on earth that can deny that he has earned the right to citizenship."

flight easy for those wishing to escape, persuaded many slave owners to sell their slaves farther south. Although slavery was not as deeply entrenched in the culture of the border states, the majority of whites—driven mostly by racist fears—were in favor of maintaining slavery.

Because there was so much sympathy for the Confederacy in the border states, there was danger that at any time they might secede, which would greatly reduce the chances of a Union victory. The possibility of Maryland seceding was particularly worrisome. The only lines for overland supplies and transportation to Washington, D.C., ran through Maryland. If Maryland seceded, the nation's capital would be surrounded by rebellious states.

Lincoln and his cabinet, though, were worried that black Union soldiers would prompt the Border States to secede.

Shortly after the Union soldiers surrendered at Fort Sumter, pro-Confederate riots broke out in Maryland. An angry mob attacked a group of Union troops passing through Baltimore. The soldiers panicked and fired into the crowd, killing twelve civilians. Confederate sympathizers in Maryland retaliated by cutting Union telegraph wires and burning bridges.

Lincoln responded to the chaos by authorizing Union general Winfield Scott to suspend the writ of habeas corpus between Philadelphia and Washington, D.C., if necessary for public safety.

In authorizing the writ to be suspended, Lincoln allowed Union soldiers to detain without trial anyone suspected of

One of the many protections in the U.S. Constitution against loss of liberty at the hands of the government is the writ of habeas corpus. Habeas corpus is Latin for "you shall have the body" and refers to the government summoning a person for questioning or holding a person without a trial. The writ of habeas corpus allows citizens to appeal to a court of law if they feel that they are being detained unjustly.

causing unrest. On May 25, Union soldiers arrested Maryland politician John Merryman for recruiting and training Confederate soldiers. Merryman's lawyers took their complaint against Lincoln to the Supreme Court, arguing that the president didn't have the power to suspend the writ. Chief Justice Roger Taney agreed with Merryman, ruling that only Congress had the authority to suspend the writ—a conclusion accepted as true today by constitutional scholars. Lincoln ignored the Supreme Court ruling, insisting that his presidential war powers enabled him to suspend the rules to put down the rebellion in the South. His actions allowed his enemies to paint him as a tyrant bent on trampling personal liberty in America.

Civil war meant that the enemy was literally within U.S.

Article I, Section 9 of the Constitution provides for the writ to be suspended "when in Cases of Rebellion or Invasion the public Safety may require it." The problem was that Article I defined congressional powers, not presidential powers, raising the question of whether Lincoln had the authority as president to suspend the writ.

borders. This was particularly true in the border states where loyalties—even within families—were divided. Mary Lincoln experienced firsthand the heartbreak of a divided family. Her own brother, George Todd, and her half brothers, Alexander Todd, David Todd, and Samuel Todd all joined the Confederate army, as did her half sister Emilie's husband.

Almost immediately after fighting broke out, enslaved people ran away and poured across Union lines and into Union army camps. Initially, generals returned the fugitives to their masters. They did so because the Constitution required it, and because they were afraid of angering the Border States.

In May of 1861, three runaway blacks arrived at General Butler's post at Fort Monroe in Virginia. Their owners demanded the return of their "property." Butler, playing on the absurdity of calling human beings property, got the idea to declare the runaways *contraband*—a word that usually refers to illegally imported goods that the government has the right to seize. If these people were indeed property, Butler reasoned, why shouldn't he seize them as contraband? Within two months he had nine hundred "contrabands" in his camps.

Meanwhile, the vice president and others were urging Lincoln to immediately free *all* those enslaved and cast the war as a contest between slavery and freedom. Lincoln listened politely. He understood the wisdom of such a strategy. "I cannot imagine that any European power would dare to recognize and aid the Southern Confederacy," he told a White House visitor, "if it becomes clear that the Confederacy stands for slavery and the Union for freedom." But Lincoln remained convinced that the public was not ready for emancipation. He also believed that while millions of Northern Democrats were willing to fight to save the Union, many of them would not be willing to wage a war on behalf of black freedom.

He developed the habit of answering questions with stories—which baffled and irritated people who wanted straight answers. When a visitor to the White House urged Lincoln to compromise with the South, Lincoln told him Aesop's fable about a lion in love with a beautiful girl. The girl's parents refused to let her wed the lion, claiming that they feared for her safety. Because their daughter was delicate, they asked the lion to cut off his claws and teeth. The moment the lion did so, the girl's parents picked up clubs and beat the lion to death. The visitor remarked that, "it was an exceedingly interesting anecdote, and very apropos, but not altogether a satisfactory answer."

When another visitor tried to push Lincoln on emancipation, he explained that they had to be cautious because if not "we shall be like the barber out in Illinois, who was shaving a fellow with a hatchet face and lantern jaws like mine. The barber stuck his finger in his customer's mouth, to make his cheek stick out, but while shaving away he cut through the fellow's cheek and cut off his own finger!"

Abolitionist George Templeton Strong visited the White House and also tried to push Lincoln toward emancipation. Lincoln replied that he was reminded of a story: When he was a boy he and a group of friends knew they'd have to cross a rapid and dangerous river. They got to talking about how they'd cross the river when they got there. Soon they were arguing heatedly about it, until at last one of the boys said, "This here talk ain't no use. I never cross a river until I come to it."

Lincoln became a master of evasion, foot-dragging, and doublespeak. Sometimes he made statements to soothe the slaveholding border states. At other times he made statements to please the abolitionists. He ended up frustrating all sides. He enflamed the South by talking about the evils of slavery. He enraged abolitionists and black activists by implying that slave owners in the border states should be allowed to keep their slaves and repeating concerns blacks and whites will be unable to live together as equals.

He ignored all criticism. "If I were to try to read, much less answer, all the attacks made on me, this shop might as well be closed for any other business. I do the very best I know how—the very best I can; and I mean to keep doing so until the end. If the end brings me out all right, what's said against me won't amount to anything. If the end brings me out wrong, ten angels swearing I was right would make no difference."

Review of Federal troops on the 4th of July by President Lincoln and General Scott; the Garibaldi Guard filing past, by Frank Vizetelly, 1861. Published in *The Illustrated London News,* August 3, 1861.

Despite the defeat at Fort Sumter, many Northerners were confident of a swift and decisive Union victory. After all, the North controlled almost all the nation's heavy industry.

Northerners outnumbered Southerners. How hard could it be for the North to blockade and starve the South into submission? Lincoln, though, was doubtful. He understood that the federal government had no cash, so he asked Congress to impose an income tax. Congress agreed to impose a tax on the highest earners. Lincoln signed the Revenue Act into law on August 5, 1861, thereby creating the nation's first income tax.

What happened next stunned the North: The Union Army suffered a humiliating defeat at the Battle of First Manassas (Bull Run) in Virginia, the first major battle of the Civil War and the only major battle fought in 1861. Lincoln blamed the defeat on Brigadier General Irvin McDowell, who many believed unequal to the task of leading the Union to victory. Lincoln removed McDowell after the battle and replaced him with George B. McClellan, a Pennsylvania Democrat to whom Lincoln gave the task of training and organizing the troops entrusted with defending Washington, D.C.

The casualties at Bull Run totaled 4,878. Many in the North now understood that the war could be lengthy and bloody—and that the outcome was uncertain.

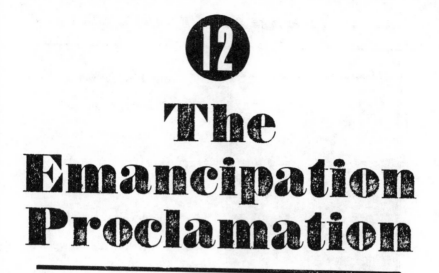

12

The Emancipation Proclamation

I hope to stand firm enough to not go backward, and yet not go forward fast enough to wreck the country's cause.

—*Abraham Lincoln*

lready by early 1862, Lincoln was becoming impatient with General McClellan. Each time Lincoln felt McClellan should attack, McClellan insisted that the time was not yet right, and his army not yet ready. Then on January 27, Lincoln issued a direct order for McClellan to march against the "insurgent forces" of the Confederacy. Still McClellan did nothing. He also made clear his contempt for the president, whom he called an idiot.

Major General McClellan, by Gibson and Company, 1862

While Lincoln was seething with frustration over his general's reluctance to fight, tragedy struck the White House. Willie Lincoln, who was then eleven years old, fell ill with a fever. A few weeks later, Tad also came down with the fever. Frantic, both Lincoln and Mary were up with the sick children night after night. Willie grew weaker. On February 20, 1862, Lincoln stepped into his office and said to his principal White House secretary, "Well, Nicolay, my boy is gone—he is actually gone!" He burst into tears. Mary sank into inconsolable grief. She was unable to attend the funeral or look after Tad, who was regaining his strength. All social activity at the White House stopped, and for months the mere mention of Willie's name would send Mary into such fits of weeping that Lincoln hired a nurse to look after her. Lincoln coped with the depression that threatened to engulf him as he always had—he threw himself into his work.

★ ★ ★ ★ ★ ★ ★ ★ ★ ★ ★ ★ ★ ★

That same month, the Union celebrated a military victory in western Tennessee when General Ulysses Grant, a native of Ohio, captured Fort Henry on the Tennessee River. Grant then advanced to Fort Donelson on the Cumberland River. He surrounded the fort with twenty-five thousand men. After several attacks and skirmishes, he captured the fort, earning the nickname "Unconditional Surrender Grant." His philosophy of war was simple: "Find out where your enemy is. Get at him as soon as you can. Strike him as hard as you can, and keep moving on." Lincoln recognized Grant as the general he needed, and promoted him to major general.

General Grant, photographed between 1860 and 1870, photographer unknown

When members of Congress learned that the Confederates were using slave labor to dig ditches for the army and cook meals, they took action. Following General Butler's example of declaring such slaves to be contraband of war, Congress passed the first Confiscation Act, allowing the government to seize rebel "property." The idea was to free any enslaved people who the

Confederate army were using as soldiers or support workers like cooks or ditch diggers. On August 6, 1862, Lincoln signed the act into law. It was the nation's document freeing slaves, but it was limited in that it only allowed the Union army to set free any slaves being used to help the rebellion.

Congress next passed the Compensated Emancipation Act outlawing slavery in Washington, D.C. The act offered up to three hundred dollars compensation to the slave owners. The act also offered the freed blacks compensation if they would emigrate to

Storming of Fort Donelson, by William Momberger, 1862. Print shows Union and Confederate soldiers in hand-to-hand combat at Fort Donelson.

another country, reflecting the widespread belief that the majority
of whites would never accept blacks as fellow citizens.

Democrats and delegates from the border states offered
the predictable objections to the act. They claimed the federal
government had no authority to abolish slavery in the nation's
capital without approval of a majority of voters. They warned
that if slaves were emancipated, race wars would erupt. Without
slavery and the highly profitable slave trade, they warned that
the capital's economy would be ruined.

Lincoln never doubted the federal government's power to abolish slavery in the nation's capital. He signed the bill into law on April 16, 1862. Abolitionist leader Frederick Douglass hailed the act as "that first step toward that righteousness which exalts a nation." Three days after Lincoln signed the act, the African Americans of Washington, D.C. held an enormous celebration. Thousands of people marched up Pennsylvania Avenue, with thousands more cheering.

Celebration of the Abolition of Slavery in the District of Columbia, by Frederick Dielman. Published in *Harper's Weekly*, May 12, 1866.

Next Lincoln signed into law the Militia Act of 1862 allowing blacks to serve in the Union army, sparking another round of celebrations from the black population in the capital. When the usual cries arose that blacks could not fight alongside whites, Lincoln put down his foot. "I have made up my mind to give the black man every possible encouragement to fight for us. I will do him justice, and I will dismiss any officer who will not carry out my policy."

By the end of the Civil War, roughly one hundred and eighty thousand blacks served in the Union army and roughly nineteen thousand in the navy. Black soldiers made up almost ten percent of the entire Union forces. Although racial prejudice among white soldiers prevented blacks from serving in combat as much as they might have, by the end of the war, sixteen black soldiers had been awarded the Medal of Honor for their valor. Black women served as nurses, spies, and scouts.

What Lincoln did next frustrated the abolitionists. General John C. Fremont, fighting in Missouri, established martial law and ordered all slaves owned by people directly rebelling against the government to be set free. Although born a Southerner, Fremont despised slavery. Lincoln stepped in and overturned the order. When another Union general, David Hunter, ordered all those enslaved in Florida, Georgia, and South Carolina to be set free, Lincoln stopped him as well. He had two reasons: there was nothing in the Constitution giving such power to generals, and Lincoln feared that Fremont and Hunter's actions would turn the border states against the Union.

While General Grant was celebrating Union victories in the West, General McClellan in the East suffered a humiliating defeat in what came to be called the Peninsula Campaign in Richmond, Virginia. The problem was that McClellan— commanding the largest army in American history— hesitated, allowing Confederate Robert E. Lee to take the initiative, attack the Union army, and beat them badly.

Another general who frustrated Lincoln was John Pope, a Kentucky-born general who was aggressive, but not very good with strategy. His letters to the president were often written from his "headquarters in the saddle." When the Union experienced a crushing defeat at the Second Battle of Bull Run in August of 1861, General McClellan was held responsible. Lincoln took no steps, though, to replace him. He believed he stood a better chance of keeping the loyalty of Northern Democrats and border states if some of their own were in positions of power.

Although the Civil War absorbed most of Lincoln's attention, he found time to work on internal improvements. In keeping with his deeply held belief that the federal government must work to better the lives of its citizens, he established the Department of Agriculture on May 15, 1862. With his own rural background in pioneer farming, he understood well the needs of the farmer. He envisioned the new department bringing the latest improvements in technology to the farmer and seeking ways to serve their interests. Soon afterward, on July 1, 1862, he signed the Pacific Railway Act to construct a railroad and telegraph line from the Missouri River to the Pacific Ocean. Republicans cheered a government actively protecting the interests of the citizens. Democrats were enraged to see the power of the federal government expanding.

By the summer of 1862, with the war in its second year, Lincoln was ready to talk about issuing a general Emancipation

Proclamation. Because the president did not have executive power to free the slaves, he drafted his Emancipation Proclamation as a war measure. He was aware that any such proclamation he might issue would be limited, and would probably not have a lasting effect. A later president could repeal the proclamation, or the Supreme Court could overturn it. Moreover, because the proclamation was an emergency war measure, it would free only the slaves in the Confederate states.

He showed a draft to his cabinet on July 22, 1862. Secretary of State Seward advised Lincoln to issue the proclamation after a Union victory so that the proclamation would appear to come from strength instead of weakness. Lincoln agreed to wait.

The Emancipation Proclamation

About a month later, on August 14, 1862. Lincoln called a meeting of black leaders to the White House. Lincoln did not tell them that a general Emancipation Proclamation was in the works. Instead he suggested colonization—the slaves should be freed and sent to live elsewhere, perhaps Africa or the Caribbean or farther west.

The black leaders angrily rejected the idea. After the meeting, Frederick Douglass called Lincoln "a genuine representative of American prejudice," and accused him of being more concerned about the border states than any principle of "justice and humanity." The editor of the *Pacific Appeal*, a leading black newspaper, said it was evident that the president and his cabinet "cared but little for justice to the negro." Because of the timing of the meeting and because there was nothing in Lincoln's Emancipation Proclamation about colonization, some historians concluded that Lincoln called the meeting to prepare the white population for the coming proclamation, because the idea of colonization would make black freedom more acceptable to those whites who insisted the two races could not live together as equals.

The First Reading of the Emancipation Proclamation Before the Cabinet, by Francis Bicknell Carpenter, 1866

Shortly after the meeting, Confederate General Lee mounted an invasion of Maryland. Early on the morning of September 17, 1862, General McClellan led the Union army to defend Maryland. McClellan faced the Confederates near Antietam Creek

in Maryland. The armies engaged in an epic battle that turned out to be the bloodiest single day in United States history. Before the day was over, almost twenty-three thousand soldiers were wounded with almost four thousand dead.

The two armies fought to a standstill—then the Confederate army retreated. McClellan allowed them to retreat instead of

General Robert E. Lee,
by Julian Vannerson, 1864

delivering a final blow that Lincoln believed might have ended the war. McClellan's excuse exasperated Lincoln. He said he let the Confederates retreat because his army needed time to rest and refit.

The battle, though, could still be called a Union victory—at least enough to give Lincoln an opportunity to issue the first order of Emancipation Proclamation. Five days later, on September 23,

The Emancipation Proclamation

Lincoln issued a preliminary Emancipation Proclamation declaring that as of January 1, 1863, all those enslaved in the rebellious states "shall be then, thenceforward, and forever free."

Frederick Douglass responded by writing, "We shout for joy that we live to record this righteous decree." Douglass acknowledged that although the president might be slow, he was "not the man to reconsider, retract and contradict words and purposes solemnly proclaimed over his official signature." Abolitionist William Lloyd Garrison said the document was an occasion for great rejoicing, but he objected to its limited scope—it did not free those enslaved in the border states. Other abolitionists complained that the document didn't contain a moral censure of slavery.

Slave owners were enraged. A newspaper in Louisville, Kentucky wrote, "the President has as much right to abolish the institution of marriage, or the laws of a State regulating the relation of parent and child, as to nullify the right of a State to regulate the relations of the white and black races." Confederates called Lincoln a dictator and fanatic who must be stopped by any means, including "revolution or private assassination." Jefferson Davis, president of the Confederacy, who believed that without masters driving them those enslaved would starve, understood the proclamation as "a measure by which several millions of human beings of an inferior race, peaceful and contented laborers in their sphere, are doomed to extermination."

Lincoln ignored the criticism. He had a larger problem on his hands. McClellan was still ignoring his orders to pursue the Confederates in their retreat from Antietam Creek. In mid-October—a month after the battle—Lincoln received a dispatch from General McClellan explaining that he wasn't pressing forward because his horses were fatigued. "Will you pardon me for asking," Lincoln shot back, "what the horses of your army have done since the battle of Antietam that fatigue anything?"

Lincoln, entirely out of patience, wanted to fire him—even though doing so might antagonize the Northern Democrats. He waited, though, until after the midterm elections.

During the midterm election, Former Ohio governor William Allen, following the Democratic strategy of stirring up racist fears, warned Ohioans that if they didn't vote Democratic, one million freed slaves "with their hands reeking in the blood of murdered women and children," would "cross over into our state looking for work." After the votes were counted, Democrats picked up an additional thirty-four seats in the House of Representatives. Because the South was not represented, Republicans held on to a narrow majority. With the midterms behind him, Lincoln fired

McClellan and in his place appointed General Ambrose Burnside. Burnside proved equally disastrous after leading the Union army of the Potomac to defeat at the Battle of Fredericksburg.

✷　✷　✷　✷　✷　✷　✷　✷　✷　✷　✷　✷　✷　✷　✷

To finance the war and strengthen the Union's economy— and to implement more Henry Clay–type internal improvements—Lincoln signed into law the National Bank Act of 1863, a piece of legislation designed to create a national banking system. The act also designed a uniform national currency—until then, each state had its own currency—and raised funds by selling government securities.

Selling securities allows a government to raise money by encouraging individuals to invest in the government. The government sells bonds to individuals or businesses and pays interest over time. Selling government bonds essentially allows the government to borrow money from citizens and foreign investors. The result is a continuous source of revenue for the government, usually accompanied by a long-term national debt.

By early 1863, the North was growing depressed and war-weary. The number of dead and wounded was stunning, and the end of the war was nowhere in sight. The failure of the Union army to secure a decisive victory tormented Lincoln.

Looking careworn, anxious, and very pale, Lincoln frequently visited the troops. When a country boy from Vermont was sentenced to die for falling asleep in sentry duty, Lincoln pardoned him. When a nineteen-year-old was found guilty of desertion, a Congressman urged Lincoln to let the execution go forward as an example, but Lincoln refused, saying, "When I think of these mere lads, who had never before left their homes, enlisting . . . I have so much sympathy I cannot condemn him to die for forgetting the obligations of the soldier and longing for home life." He pardoned another deserter, saying, "Let him fight instead of being shot." Officers complained that the president's steady stream of pardons and reprieves undermined discipline, but Lincoln continued to issue pardons.

In late June of 1863, Confederate General Robert E. Lee marched his army into Pennsylvania. The Union army led by General George Meade set out to stop him. With the major roads in southern Pennsylvania leading to a town named Gettysburg, there the two armies met. The fighting near Gettysburg was fierce and bloody, lasting three days. The losses on both sides were stagger-ing: thirty-one hundred Unions soldiers and thirty-nine hundred Confederate soldiers lay dead. Another thirty-three thousand were wounded.

On July 3, the Confederates, finding themselves under attack from three sides, were weakened and weary. The next day, Lee took advantage of a heavy rain to retreat toward Virginia. It was a clear Union victory and a much needed one. But the victory was blunted when General Meade allowed Lee to retreat. Capturing Lee might have decisively ended the war. Lincoln immediately criticized Meade for his failure and grieved over Lee's escape.

Meanwhile, General Grant was scoring victories in the West, where his military objective was to gain control of the Mississippi River. For months Grant had been trying to capture Vicksburg, Mississippi, a city vital to his effort. After being besieged by Grant for two months, Vicksburg surrendered to him on July 4.

The victories at Gettysburg and Vicksburg marked a turning point in the war. With a Union victory within reach, Lincoln's pop-ularity soared. Lincoln's temperament—his inclination toward cool reason and long deliberation, his nuanced and sometimes ambig-uous answers, and his ability to play to all sides at once—seemed to Northern observers gentle and wise, the mark of a man with a

Battle of Gettysburg, by Wm. C. Robertson, 1867

deep intellect. One euphoric abolitionist predicted that Lincoln's "historic heights will dwarf all others in our annals."

But there was still much work to be done. The South vowed to fight to the end. In the words of Lincoln's White House secretary, the "tiger is wounded unto death, but it will die hard, and fight to the last." Lincoln believed that victory would require crushing the South, and then building it back up and drawing it back into the Union.

Because Mary Lincoln's family was largely pro-Confederacy, she suffered deeply, feeling the divisions in her own family keenly. Once, a visiting friend was shocked when Mary said she wished her brothers fighting for the Confederacy would be captured or killed. When the friend protested, Mary explained, "They would kill my husband if they could, and destroy our Government—the dearest of all things to us."

When word came that Mary's brother-in-law, husband to her favorite half sister, Emilie, died fighting for the Confederacy in the Battle of Chickamauga, both Lincoln and Mary grieved. Mary wanted her sister to be allowed to visit the White House, so Lincoln granted Mary's sister a pass to travel across Union lines. Emilie stayed at the White House for two weeks, drawing ire from those who questioned Mary's patriotism to the Union.

Mary's popularity was at an all-time low. Her extravagant

spending—she felt the White House needed repairs and upgrades to honor the office of the president, and she loved wearing expensive clothing—brought her criticism from all sides. Southerners scorned her as a traitor to her home state and land of her birth. Northerners suspected her of being disloyal to the Union because she had close relatives in the Confederate army. After reading scathing commentary of herself in the newspaper, she turned to her sister Emilie, who was then visiting, and commented that she was the scapegoat for both North and South.

While Lincoln often complained in private about his wife, he was gallant in public. "My wife is as handsome as when she was a girl," Lincoln said once at a White House reception, "and I, a poor nobody then, fell in love with her; and what is more, I have never fallen out."

✶ ✶ ✶ ✶ ✶ ✶ ✶ ✶ ✶ ✶ ✶ ✶ ✶ ✶ ✶

A young lawyer in Gettysburg, David Wills, took on the project of creating a national cemetery for the soldiers killed on the Gettysburg battlefield. Wills scheduled the consecration ceremony for November 19, 1863, and invited Lincoln to speak. Lincoln accepted, and penned the speech that established him as one of the gifted writers of his age. His love of poetry helped him create a speech with the cadence and rhythm that made it memorable—and easy to memorize. His speech began with:

Four score and seven years ago our fathers brought forth on this continent, a new nation, conceived in liberty, and dedicated to the proposition that all men are created equal.

And ended with his hope that the nation would have a new birth of freedom:

. . . we here highly resolve that these dead shall not have died in vain—that this nation, under God, shall have a new

Lincoln at Gettysburg, by Fletcher C. Ransom, 1938

birth of freedom—and that government of the people, by the people, for the people, shall not perish from the earth.

The *Ohio State Journal* reported that Lincoln's "calm but earnest utterance of this deep and beautiful address stirred the deepest fountains of feeling and emotion in the hearts of the vast throngs before him; and when he had concluded, scarcely could an untearful eye be seen, while sobs of smothered emotion were heard on every hand."

While the North applauded the speech, the South sharply criticized it. Southern newspapers insisted that the war was not being fought over slavery—the Confederate view was that the war was being fought to maintain the existing government and Constitution as handed down by the Founding Fathers. Confederates objected to Lincoln's statement that the nation was founded on the idea that all men were created equal, pointing out that the Constitution said not one word about all men being equal, and in fact, with the three-fifths rule and other proslavery portions of the Constitution, the Constitution expressly admitted that the races were unequal. Many in the South believed that the real cause of the war was that the North was jealous of the South's wealth and prosperity.

A New Birth
of Freedom

As I would not be a slave, so I would not be a master.
This expresses my idea of democracy. Whatever differs from
this, to the extent of the difference, is no democracy.

— Abraham Lincoln

n February of 1864, Lincoln promoted General Ulysses S. Grant to lieutenant general, making Grant the first to hold that title since George Washington. He then elevated General William Tecumseh Sherman, a native of Ohio, into Grant's former position.

Sherman had the reputation of being as fierce as Grant, and as brilliant a strategist.

With the war having turned so far in the Union's favor, the South understood that it could not hope for victory on the battlefield. The only hope was to keep fighting for a negotiated peace that would keep the South intact—slavery and all. Sherman, though, like Lincoln, believed that the nation could not continue half slave and half free. Given the tenacity of the South, Sherman believed the only way to wrest an unconditional surrender was to entirely break the morale of the Confederacy and destroy all Southern desire to wage war. Sherman and Grant worked on a strategy that would cripple the Confederate States of America.

General William Tecumseh Sherman, photographed between 1860 and 1875, photographer unknown

Meanwhile, changes were taking place in the North. Three long and bloody years of war prompted a growing desire among Northerners to abolish slavery once and for all. Before the Civil War, abolitionism never caught on with the majority of voters, even in the North. The Liberty Party, the official party of the abolitionists, never won a majority in a single county in any presidential race. *The Liberator*, the abolitionist newspaper, had a circulation under three thousand. Now abolitionism was catching on. Many Northerners had tolerated slavery, believing that allowing slavery in the South was the only way to hold the United States together—but after three years of war, it now seemed that the only way to hold the Union together was to put an end to the furious and bitter debate over slavery by getting rid of the institution altogether. In addition, the war allowed many Northerners to see up close, for the first time, the horrors of slavery. One modern scholar suggested that the burgeoning abolition fever was partly a vindictive desire to punish the South for the war. Others suggested that seeing the courage of the black soldiers convinced many whites that blacks were indeed fit for full citizenship.

Women's groups led by abolitionists Elizabeth Cady Stanton and Susan B. Anthony drummed up support for emancipation by circulating petitions. Women throughout the North took up the

cause. Abolitionism, which had earlier been the movement of a few fringe radicals, now moved into the mainstream.

Along with growing abolitionism came a widespread belief in the North that the Constitution was flawed and needed to be fixed. Previously, reverence for the Founding Fathers and the Constitution made the document almost untouchable—but only a constitutional amendment could overturn *Dred Scott v. Sandford* and abolish slavery. Ironically, some of the earliest supporters of such an amendment were the same leaders of the Northern Democratic Party who had opposed the Emancipation Proclamation. But slavery no longer had widespread support, and Northern Democrats didn't want their party bogged down by an unpopular position. The problem was convincing voters, who for years had been told that reverence for the Founding Fathers meant it was best to keep the Constitution as they had written it.

In January of 1864, the Senate Judiciary Committee began meeting to draft a constitutional amendment. The final draft of the amendment read:

Section 1. Neither slavery nor involuntary servitude, except as a punishment for crime whereof the party shall have

Elizabeth Cady Stanton and Susan B. Anthony, by Napoleon Sarony, 1870

been duly convicted, shall exist within the United States,
or any place subject to their jurisdiction.

Section 2. Congress shall have the power to enforce this
article by appropriate legislation.

The Amendment went first to the Senate. With the South not represented in the Senate, the amendment passed easily. The amendment went next to the House of Representatives, where opposition from some Northern Democrats was so strong the amendment seemed doomed to fail.

★ ★ ★ ★ ★ ★ ★ ★ ★ ★ ★ ★ ★ ★

By the summer of 1864 it was time to prepare for the next presidential election. The Republicans once more held their convention in Chicago. On May 18, they nominated Lincoln for reelection. This time, though, his vice president would be Andrew Johnson—a Democrat from Tennessee who Lincoln had appointed military governor of Tennessee after the Confederate portions of the state were taken back by Union armies. Lincoln and Johnson ran on a promise to end the war with a powerful military campaign, the unconditional surrender by the South, and an end to slavery once and for all.

While the Democrats prepared for their convention, President Lincoln signed the Yosemite Valley Grant Act, setting aside large stretches of land in California for national parks. For the first time the federal government retained ownership of scenic lands for the purpose of protecting them and allowing all people to enjoy them.

The Democrats also held their convention in Chicago. They met in August and nominated former general George McClellan—the general Lincoln had fired because his fight against the Confederates had seemed half-hearted. McClellan's running mate, Ohio Congressman George Pendleton, had opposed the war from the beginning and voted against supplies for the Union army.

The Democrats devised what they called a peace platform, promising a speedy end to the war by entering peace negotiations with the South. They called four years of war a failure in which the Constitution was continually disregarded. Although they avoided mentioning slavery, they ran on a promise to preserve the Constitution as the Founding Fathers had ratified it. Senator Lazarus Powell from Kentucky, voicing the opinion of many, said, "I believe this government was made by white men and for white men; and if it is ever to be preserved it must be preserved by white men." He added, "The white man is superior and will be so whether you call [the black man] a slave or an equal. It has ever been so, and I can see no reason why the history of all the past shall be reversed."

After the campaigns were under way, Lincoln received a letter from a Pennsylvanian saying, "Equal Rights & Justice to all white men in the United States forever. White men is in class number one & black men is in class number two & must be governed by white men forever." Lincoln, moved to sarcasm, posed as his own secretary, and wrote back: "The President has received yours of yesterday, and is kindly paying attention to it. As it is my business to assist him whenever I can, I will thank you to inform me, for his use, whether you are either a white man or black one, because in either case, you cannot be regarded as an entirely impartial judge."

Lincoln's prospects for reelection did not look good, even though he was widely praised by Northerners. The *New York Evening Post*, which had initially been skeptical about Lincoln, now proclaimed that he "has gained wisdom by experience. Every year has seen our cause more successful; every year has seen abler generals, more skillful leaders, called to the head; every year has seen fewer errors, greater ability, greater energy, in the administration of affairs. . . . While Mr. Lincoln stays in power, this healthy and beneficial state of things will continue."

The problem was that the Democratic promise of a negotiated peace and speedy end to the fighting held much appeal for
a war-weary North. Fearful that if McClellan became president,
he would immediately repeal the Emancipation Proclamation,
Lincoln met with Frederick Douglass on August 19, 1864. Douglass entered Lincoln's office to find the president in an "alarmed
condition." Lincoln told Douglass he was afraid he was about to
lose the election because of Northern opposition to the war, so he
wanted to move as many enslaved men, women, and children as
possible across Union lines where they might retain their freedom
should McClellan win the presidency. "The slaves are not coming
so rapidly and numerously as I had hoped," Lincoln told Douglass. Douglass replied that, "slave holders know how to keep such
things from their slaves." Lincoln then told him, "I want you to
set about devising some means of making them acquainted with
it, and for bringing them into our lines." Douglass "listened with
the deepest interest and profoundest satisfaction," and agreed
to organize a handful of scouts who would inform those enslaved
of the need to come within Union boundaries.

★ ★ ★ ★ ★ ★ ★ ★ ★ ★ ★ ★ ★ ★ ★

Sherman's March to the Sea, by Alexander Hay Ritchie, 1868

On September 1, 1864, General Sherman captured Atlanta, a railroad hub and the industrial center of the Confederacy. It was a major Union victory. Sherman's plan was to march from Atlanta to the sea with sixty thousand soldiers, cutting a two-hundred-eighty-five-mile-wide swath through Georgia, destroying everything in his path, including all means of transportation. His goal was to secure an unconditional surrender by splitting the Confederacy in half, and forcing the rebels to feel the terrifying hand of the war.

Sherman's armies marched through Georgia, burning and plundering. Although Sherman's soldiers did not destroy towns, they took food and livestock and burned the houses and barns of anyone who fought back. As his army marched, thousands of enslaved men, women, and children followed in their wake, flocking to Union camps. Many were able to make it to freedom. Others were captured by the Confederate army, faced hostility from racist Union soldiers, or did not survive the brutal march.

Sherman's success assured the North of a quick and resounding victory, undermining the Democratic campaign slogan that the war was a failure. The following month, as part of the amendment fever sweeping parts of the nation, Maryland voters ratified a new constitution abolishing slavery in the state. The vote was close—50.3 percent to 49.7 percent—illustrating the strength of proslavery feeling in the border states, but it was a victory for black freedom.

The 1864 presidential election was held on November 8. Lincoln waited at the War Department telegraph room for news. The first victory came from Maryland, where the Republicans scored a solid ten thousand–vote victory. Upon hearing the news, Lincoln "smiled good-naturedly and said that was a fair beginning." When Pennsylvania also went heavily Republican, the outcome was clear. Lincoln quipped that, "As goes Pennsylvania, so goes the Union, they say."

With the Confederate states not participating in the election,

Lincoln won with 55.03 percent of the popular vote, losing only Kentucky, Delaware, and New Jersey. Although many Confederates understood that Lincoln's reelection meant their cause was doomed, Confederate president Jefferson Davis greeted the news by vowing to keep fighting.

Not long afterward, on December 21, Sherman's troops arrived in Savannah. The city was undefended and fell easily. Sherman presented the city, with twenty-five thousand bales of cotton, to Lincoln as an early Christmas gift.

✦ ✦ ✦ ✦ ✦ ✦ ✦ ✦ ✦ ✦ ✦ ✦ ✦ ✦ ✦

With the election behind him, Lincoln turned to his first major postelection goal: Get the Thirteenth Amendment abolishing slavery passed and ratified. He threw all his weight behind the amendment. Because it was clear the Confederacy would not achieve independence and was fighting on for a negotiated peace, Lincoln argued that adopting the amendment would shorten the war by giving the Confederacy less reason to continue fighting. He then went to work persuading enough House Democrats to switch their votes so that the amendment might pass. One congressman from Ohio changed his mind and voted for the amendment because he wanted the issue of slavery resolved once and for all. For too long it had been the cause of division. When Lincoln still needed two more votes, he told supporters in the House of Representatives that the two additional votes must be obtained by "hook or crook"—a comment that has been interpreted as a willingness to employ any means, whether legal or not. Rumors were afloat that radicals in New York were offering hefty bribes to Democrats who were willing to vote for the amendment.

As the hour for voting on the amendment drew near, a rumor swept through the House of Representatives that Confederate peace commissioners were on their way to Washington, no doubt hoping to offer peace in exchange for stopping the amendment from passing. The rumor was wrong in one particular detail: As Lincoln knew, the peace commissioners were on their way to Hampton Roads, Virginia, not Washington, where they would meet with Seward. Lincoln "calmed the storm" in the House by assuring everyone in writing: "As far as I know, there are no peace commissioners in this city, or likely to be in it." The lawyerly hairsplitting amused Lincoln and didn't trouble his conscience for a moment.

The vote was taken, and the amendment won one hundred nineteen to fifty-six. When the results were announced, there was a stunned silence in the chamber, followed by an explosion of

Scene in the House on the Passage of the Proposition to Amend the Constitution, January 31, 1865. Celebrating the passage of the Thirteenth Amendment, from the cover of *Harper's Weekly*, February 18, 1865.

cheers, with congressmen throwing their hats up, catching them, and slapping them against their desk. The women, who thronged the galleries, waved handkerchiefs and wept.

While there is no evidence that Lincoln personally offered rewards in exchange for votes, there is evidence that Seward and other passionate abolitionists in Lincoln's administration did. A congressman from Kentucky, George Yeaman, who had been elected out of office and was finishing his term, previously voted against the amendment. Now he switched his vote. After leaving office, he was named minister to Denmark. A Democrat from Brooklyn also switched his vote—and later when he was out of office, he was given the coveted post of naval agent in New York.

Seward's meeting with the peace conference in Virginia got off to a bad start when the Confederates arrived prepared to negotiate a peace between the *two separate* countries—a plucky and defiant position given that the South was taking a major beating in the war with no hope of winning. Lincoln wasn't about to recognize the Confederacy as a separate country, so the only agreement reached was over a prisoner-of-war exchange.

The Thirteenth Amendment next went to the states for ratification. The first of the Northern states to ratify the amendment was Illinois, on February 1, 1865. By the time of Lincoln's second inauguration on March 4, eighteen states had ratified the amendment. Nine more were needed.

✳ ✳ ✳ ✳ ✳ ✳ ✳ ✳ ✳ ✳ ✳ ✳ ✳ ✳ ✳

Meanwhile, there was turbulence in the Lincoln household. Robert, the Lincolns' oldest son, returned from a semester at Harvard Law School determined to leave his studies and join the army. He was embarrassed to be out of uniform

Robert Todd Lincoln,
Matthew Brady, 1865

while so many were laying down their lives for their country. Mary reacted with complete hysterics: She had lost two sons already and could not bear the thought of losing another. Lincoln responded with his usual calm logic. "Many a poor mother has given up all her sons," he told her, "and our son is not more dear to us than the sons of other people are to their mothers."

When she persisted, he suggested that she be less selfish. In the end they compromised: Robert was allowed to join the army, but he was given a post in General Grant's administration—a position that allowed him to wear a uniform and join the war but kept him safe. Robert was not pleased with the compromise, but he had no choice.

✳ ✳ ✳ ✳ ✳ ✳ ✳ ✳ ✳ ✳ ✳ ✳ ✳

March 4, 1865, the day of Lincoln's second inauguration, dawned dark and rainy, but crowds thronged into the plaza in front of the East Portico of the Capitol to watch the ceremony. By the time the ceremony was ready to begin, an estimated fifty thousand people had gathered to watch. The moment Lincoln stepped onto the stage, the sun broke through the heavy clouds. In the words of one journalist, "The sun, which had been obscured all day, burst forth in its unclouded meridian splendor and flooded the spectacle with glory and light."

Lincoln's speech lived up to the omen. His second inaugural address is widely considered one of his most brilliant speeches. He finally did what the radicals had wanted him to do four years earlier: He cast the Civil War as a war against slavery. He called slavery a moral offense. He added that the moral blame belonged not only to the South but to the entire nation. He said it was up to the entire nation to meet the challenge of fitting the former slaves into postwar America. He concluded with his now famous words:

With malice toward none, with charity for all, with firmness in the right as God gives us to see the right, let us strive on to finish the work we are in, to bind up the nation's wounds, to care for him who shall have borne the battle and for his widow and his orphan, to do all which may achieve and cherish a just and lasting peace among ourselves and with all nations.

After Lincoln took the oath of office, the crowed cheered, the band played, and the artillery fired a round of salutes.

That evening, the White House gates were thrown open and the public were invited to a reception. When Frederick Douglass tried to enter, two policemen stopped him, grabbed him rudely by the arm, and told him that no persons of his color were to enter. Douglass, calm now in his friendship with the president, told them there must be some mistake. After he entered, he had no trouble spotting Lincoln, for with his great height Lincoln towered over the crowd.

When Lincoln saw Douglass, he exclaimed loudly enough for people around him to hear, "Here comes my friend Douglass." Then, taking Douglass by the hand, he asked what Douglass thought of his inaugural address, adding that, "There is no man in the country whose opinion I value more than yours. I want to know what you think of it."

Modestly, Douglass said, "Mr. Lincoln, I must not detain you with my poor opinion, when there are thousands waiting to shake hands with you." When Lincoln insisted that he wanted Douglass's opinion, Douglass said, "Mr. Lincoln, that was a sacred effort."

Lincoln said, "I'm glad you liked it!" Douglass then stepped back to allow others to speak with the president.

For the first time, a black man attended a formal White House event.

* * * * * * * * * * * * * * *

One of Lincoln's first acts in his second term was to create a new federal agency, the Bureau of Refugees, Freedmen, and Abandoned Lands, to offer relief to refugees by offering medicine, food, education, and distributing abandoned lands to those in need. The agency was ordered to treat all refugees the same, whether black or white.

By early April, General Robert E. Lee's army in Virginia was in tatters. Lee tried to retreat west from Virginia to North Carolina, but the Union cavalry led by General Sheridan outran them and cut off their escape at the village of Appomattox Court House. Lee launched an attack to break through the Union forces. Unable to break through, he had no choice but to send a message to General Grant offering to surrender.

The two generals met in the parlor of a private home on April 9, 1865, at 1 p.m. In exchange for Lee's unconditional surrender, Grant allowed the Confederate soldiers to return home with their horses, which would be needed for the spring

planting. With the exception of a few minor skirmishes, the Civil War had come to an end.

After receiving news of Lee's surrender, Lincoln paused to celebrate with friends and family. He made sure though to take none of the credit for the victory, telling visitors who came to congratulate him that he wanted it understood that the honor went to the military.

Then, he turned to the difficult problem of rebuilding the South and drawing the rebellious states back into the Union. Many in Washington—and in the president's own administration—wanted to see the rebels punished. Lincoln didn't want to punish anyone. It seemed to Lincoln that protecting the former slaves was more important than punishing the former masters. He sensed that many in the North were ready to consider allowing blacks to vote—and what better way to protect the blacks than to empower them with the vote?

On April 10, crowds gathered outside the White House, joyous at Lee's surrender, clamoring for a speech. Lincoln sidestepped the request, promising a speech the next day. He intended to write out his speech—something he rarely did. But he wanted to take great care with his words, for he knew what he was about to say would be extremely important—and alarming to many. He intended to broach the subject of allowing black men to vote as equal citizens.

The following day, with Tad at his side, Lincoln stepped to the window of the White House and read his speech to a cheering crowd. After a careful buildup, he said, "It is also unsatisfactory to some that the elective franchise is not given to the colored man." It was to be Lincoln's last speech.

More than six hundred and twenty thousand American soldiers died in the Civil War—roughly two percent of the entire American population. More soldiers died in the Civil War than all other American wars combined, from the Revolutionary War until Vietnam.

Afterward

he Lincolns and their guests, Major Henry Rathbone and Clara Harris, were late to Ford's Theatre. They arrived at eight thirty, after the play started. The moment they appeared, the audience stood and cheered, and the orchestra struck up "Hail to the Chief." The Lincolns and their guests settled into their seats in the presidential box. Lincoln sat in a rocking chair made especially to accommodate his long body.

At about ten fifteen, John Wilkes Booth walked calmly up the stairs and approached the door to the presidential box. Because he was a well-known actor, nobody thought anything of his presence. The policeman on guard in the corridor had left his post, so Booth showed his identification card to Charles Forbes, a member of the White House staff. Forbes let him in. Booth entered the presidential box and locked the door behind him. He crept up behind Lincoln, drew out his Derringer gun, and at close range, fired at the back of the president's head.

John Wilkes Booth, by Alex Gardner, 1865

Lincoln slumped forward. The bullet entered behind his left ear and lodged behind his right eye. Mary, shocked by the firing of the pistol, saw the flash, screamed, and then fell into a faint. Major Rathbone leaped toward Booth, but Booth pulled out a dagger and slashed his arm. Booth then leaped over the edge of the box onto the stage. Upon landing, he shouted, "Sic semper tyrannis" (thus always to tyrants), the Virginia state motto. He broke his leg when he landed, but in the pandemonium that erupted in the theater, he escaped out the back.

The moment the bullet entered Lincoln's head, he lost consciousness and never regained it. Three doctors made their way through the chaos in the theater to the presidential box. Seeing the hole at the back of the president's head, they feared he wouldn't survive being moved back to the White House, so they had him carried to a boardinghouse across the street. A weeping Mary, having recovered from her own paralyzing shock, joined them there. She entered the house and shouted, "Where is my husband?" Upon reaching his bedside, she kissed his bleeding head and tried to get him to speak. When he remained mute, she begged for Tad, believing Lincoln would speak to the son he loved so dearly.

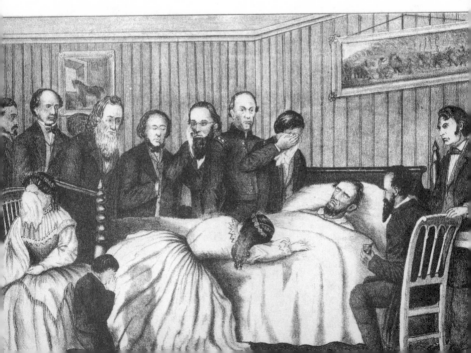

The bedroom where Lincoln lay was soon crowded with cabinet members, doctors, generals, friends, and his inconsolable family. Lincoln died at 7:22 a.m. Nine hours after the bullet entered his head, Edwin Stanton, Lincoln's secretary of war and close friend, said, "Now he belongs to the ages."

News of the president's death spread swiftly. All across the country, flags flew at half-mast and businesses closed. The next day, despite the chilly rain, weeping crowds gathered in front of the White House. When Lincoln's body lay in state in the East Room of the White House, more than twenty thousand people walked past the casket. Thousands of others gave up and left because of the long lines.

On April 21, Lincoln's body was placed in a funeral train, where it was conveyed to Springfield for burial. Meanwhile, John Wilkes Booth was on the run. Secretary of War Edwin Stanton offered an enormous reward of one hundred thousand dollars to anyone who could capture the "murderer of our late beloved president, Abraham Lincoln."

Booth was stunned by how the assassination was portrayed in the press. He had spent so much time among like-minded people who hated Lincoln, and he had read so many newspaper

Lincoln's Death Bed, by H. H. Lloyd & Co., 1865

"$100,000 REWARD!" Broadside advertising a reward for the capture of Lincoln's assassin, illustrated with photographic prints of Booth and his two conspirators, John H. Surratt and David E. Herold.

accounts denouncing Lincoln as a tyrant bent on destroying the Constitution and personal liberty, that he expected to be hailed as a hero. Instead he was stunned to learn he was being hunted down like a beast, while Lincoln was held up throughout much of the nation as a martyred saint.

On April 26, a group of Union soldiers caught up with Booth and found him hiding in a tobacco barn about sixty miles from Washington, D.C. The soldiers tried to capture him. Booth was killed in the struggle.

Afterward

✳ ✳ ✳ ✳ ✳ ✳ ✳ ✳ ✳ ✳ ✳ ✳ ✳ ✳ ✳

In November, American poet Walt Whitman paid homage to Abraham Lincoln with his poem, *O Captain! My Captain!* The final stanza reads:

> *My Captain does not answer, his lips are pale and still,*
>
> *My father does not feel my arm, he has no pulse nor will,*
>
> *The ship is anchor'd safe and sound, its voyage closed and*
> *done,*
>
> *From fearful trip the victor ship comes in with object won;*
>
> *Exult O shores, and ring O bells!*
>
> *But I with mournful tread,*
>
> *Walk the deck my Captain lies,*
>
> *Fallen cold and dead.*

Legacy

fter Lincoln's death, several more state legislatures were persuaded to ratify the Thirteenth Amendment with promises that the amendment abolished slavery as it existed before the Civil War—but did nothing else. Blacks would still not have equal rights or citizenship. Because former Confederates understood that the institution of slavery was dead, Alabama, North Carolina, and Georgia became the twenty-fifth, twenty-sixth, and twenty-seventh states to ratify the amendment. On December 6, 1865, the Thirteenth Amendment became part of the U.S. Constitution.

Almost immediately Mississippi and South Carolina enacted laws called the Black Codes to restrict the liberty of the newly freed slaves. Other states soon followed. While the

Black Codes varied somewhat from state to state, the codes generally required blacks to sign yearly labor contracts and made vagrancy—or homelessness—a crime. Blacks who left their masters but refused to sign labor contracts were arrested, convicted as vagrants, and forced into labor as convicts. Black Codes also prevented blacks from attending public schools, entering certain professions, serving on juries, or testifying in court against whites.

Many in the former Confederacy had agreed to abolish slavery because they believed that once they ratified the Thirteenth Amendment, the federal government would leave them alone. They were soon to be bitterly disappointed. Those fighting for black freedom made clear that in their view, the Thirteenth Amendment was not enough. In the words of Frederick Douglass, while those who had been enslaved "bore the irons of slavery," the freed blacks were "enclosed in the same dark dungeon." In September of 1865, Ohio congressman John Bingham delivered a speech in Cleveland insisting that *every* person in the United States should be entitled to equal treatment under the law. In January of 1866, he proposed a Fourteenth Amendment and drafted the new amendment's crucial language. The first sentence granted full citizenship to freed slaves by making anyone born in the United States automatically a citizen:

> *All persons born or naturalized in the United States . . .*
> *are citizens of the United States and of the state wherein*
> *they reside.*

Next, making sure that all citizens would be entitled to equal treatment under the law, the Fourteenth Amendment stated that:

> *No state shall make or enforce any law which shall abridge*
> *the privileges or immunities of citizens of the United*
> *States; nor shall any state deprive any person of life,*
> *liberty, or property, without due process of law; nor deny*
> *to any person within its jurisdiction the equal protection of*
> *the laws.*

Section 2 of the proposed Fourteenth Amendment added that all "male inhabitants of each state . . . being twenty-one years of age," must be allowed to vote. Congressman Bingham, in drafting the Fourteenth Amendment, intended to overrule *Dred Scott v. Sandford.* He also intended for all the protections in the Bill of Rights to apply to state governments as well as the federal government.

The outcry was predictable. Opponents insisted that the proposed Fourteenth Amendment violated the rights of states to govern themselves. Other objections came from an unexpected place: two of the leading women's rights activists, Susan B. Anthony and Elizabeth Cady Stanton, objected to the word "male" and lobbied hard to have the word deleted. Why, they demanded, should women be left out? Stanton said, "If that word 'male' be inserted, it will take us a century at least to get it out." The women were ignored. The word "male" remained. Stanton and Anthony formed the American Equal Rights Association with the goal of achieving voting rights for *all* people regardless of race, color, or gender.

Bingham presented the Fourteenth Amendment to Congress on June 13, 1866. The former Confederate states, having withdrawn their senators and representatives from Congress at the start of the war, were still not represented in Congress. The amendment thus swiftly passed both houses and then went to the states for ratification. Six of the former Union states refused to ratify the amendment: New Jersey, Ohio, Kentucky, California, Delaware, and Maryland. Ten Southern states also refused. With only seventeen of the thirty-seven states willing to ratify the amendment, it fell short of the necessary votes.

On March 2, 1867, Congress required each state in the former Confederacy to ratify the Fourteenth Amendment before it would be permitted to send senators and representatives to Congress. Getting the former Confederate states to do the bidding of the North was helped by the Third Reconstruction Act, which placed the South under military rule: Thousands of Southern government officials were removed from office and replaced with Union officers and blacks newly released from the bonds of slavery. The Union officers in charge of the South organized new elections across the former Confederacy, monitored and enforced by the U.S. Army. The new election boards permitted blacks to vote while denying the vote to large numbers of former Confederate soldiers on the grounds that they had rebelled against the government. On July 9, 1868, when South Carolina became the twenty-eighth state to ratify the Fourteenth Amendment, it became part of the Constitution.

Precincts throughout the United States, particularly in the South, still found ways to prevent black men from voting. Sometimes they used simple intimidation. Other times they passed local laws that made it difficult for black men to qualify to vote by creating requirements—such as literacy tests—that newly freed slaves could not meet.

In response, in February of 1869, Congress passed the Fifteenth Amendment, which stated that:

The right of citizens of the United States to vote shall not be denied or abridged by the United States or by any State on account of race, color, or previous condition of servitude.

As with the Fourteenth Amendment, women's groups objected to being left out. They were again ignored. Because Southern states were still under military rule, Republicans were able to push one Southern legislature after another to ratify the Fifteenth Amendment. The Fifteenth Amendment became part of the Constitution when Georgia ratified it on February 2, 1870. Two months later, Thomas Mundy Peterson became the first black man in the United States to cast a ballot under the Fifteenth Amendment when he voted in a local election in Perth Amboy, New Jersey.

Thomas Mundy Peterson, the first black man to vote under the Fifteenth Amendment. Origin of the photograph is unknown.

★   ★   ★   ★   ★   ★   ★   ★   ★   ★   ★   ★   ★

The importance of the Thirteenth, Fourteenth, and Fifteenth Amendments cannot be overstated. These amendments rewrote portions of the Constitution. States no longer had unfettered rights in how they treated people within their borders. Because the federal government had the authority to enforce the amendments, the power of the federal government was greatly increased. "We the people" now included a lot more people. The concept of paternalism received a powerful blow—but deeply ingrained attitudes do not change overnight. Because so many, particularly in the South, felt that these Amendments had been forced on them, it shouldn't have been hard to predict that a powerful resistance would arise.

★   ★   ★   ★   ★   ★   ★   ★   ★   ★   ★   ★   ★

For decades after his death, Abraham Lincoln was hailed as the "Great Emancipator," the leader who freed the slaves and paved the way for the Thirteenth, Fourteenth, and Fifteenth Amendments.

Then in the latter part of the twentieth century, people started questioning the popular view of Lincoln as the Great Emancipator. They pointed to many of Lincoln's offensive and racist statements and positions, including his earlier support for colonization. They argued that he issued the Emancipation Proclamation only after caving to pressure from those who *should* be hailed as the Great Emancipators: abolitionists and black leaders. They pronounced him a white supremacist who also opposed slavery.

More recently, a new generation of scholars, led by historian LaWanda Cox, have put forward a more nuanced interpretation of Lincoln. Cox concluded that Lincoln's foot-dragging behavior and doubletalk was *not* reluctance or ambivalence, and did not spring from notions of white supremacy. Instead, she argued that his behavior sprang from a deep understanding that moving too quickly before the population was ready could cause a backlash. As another historian explained, Lincoln "always sought the meeting point between what was right in theory and what could be achieved in practice." Lincoln saw no point in putting forward plans or proposals that couldn't possibly win popular support.

Under Cox's theory of Lincoln, which has gained wide acceptance among scholars, Lincoln was a practical statesman and not an idealist. At each stage he was willing to settle for what he could accomplish, while remaining alert for opportunities to achieve his long-desired objective of liberty and justice for all.

Abraham Lincoln, created
in 1920 by Gertrude Käsebier
from an earlier photograph.

Notes

Prologue: "Now, By God, I'll Put Him Through."

2   "thin as a beanpole and ugly as a scarecrow" Michael Burlingame, *Abraham Lincoln: A Life,* vol. 1 (Baltimore, MD: Johns Hopkins University Press, reprint edition, Kindle edition, 2012) 97.

2   "positive good" From John Calhoun's "Slavery a Positive Good" speech, delivered February 6, 1837, teachingamericanhistory.org /library/document/slavery-a-positive-good.

2–3 "This country . . . black man" Michael Burlingame, *Abraham Lincoln: A Life,* vol. 2 (Baltimore, MD: Johns Hopkins University Press, reprint edition, Kindle edition, 2012) 881.

3   "We meet this evening . . . action will be proper." Lincoln's speech delivered April 11, 1865, www.gutenberg.org/files/2659/2659 -h/2659-h.htm#link2H_4_0001.

3   "That means . . . the last speech he will ever make." Burlingame, *A Life,* vol. 2, 803.

1: A Boy on the Frontier

5   "When first my father . . . bears preyed on the swine" Abraham Lincoln, *The Collected Works of Abraham Lincoln,* vol. 1. (Springfield, IL: The Abraham Lincoln Association) 386, quod.lib.umich .edu/l/lincoln and www.gutenberg.org/files/3253/3253-h/3253-h .htm.

5   "a barren waste . . . save some little patches on the creek bottoms." David Herbert Donald, *Lincoln* (New York, NY: Simon & Schuster, 1995) 22.

6   "the very poorest people." Burlingame, *A Life:* vol. 1, 16.

6   "my toes stuck out . . . shivered with the cold." Burlingame, *A Life:*

vol. 1, 54.

7 "I am naturally anti-slavery . . . think and feel." Lincoln to Albert
Hodges, April 4, 1864. Lincoln, *Collected Works,* vol. 7, quod.lib
.umich.edu/l/lincoln.

8 "more strongly than all the others . . . mind and memory" Lincoln to
Jesse Lincoln, April 1, 1854. Lincoln, *Collected Works,* vol. 8,
quod.lib.umich.edu/l/lincoln.

9 "plain unpretending plodding man" Douglas L. Wilson and Rodney
O. Davis, eds., *Herndon's Informants: Letters, Interviews, and
Statements about Abraham Lincoln* (Chicago, IL: University of Illinois
Press, 1998) 67.

9–10 "a woman known . . . in every way." Wilson and Davis,
Herndon's Informants, 113.

12 "the trees . . . twentieth year." Speech at Indianapolis,
Indiana, Sept. 19, 1859. Lincoln, *Collected Works,* vol. 3, 463.

13 "I have no wife . . . straight off." Burlingame, vol. 1, p. 27.

13 "wild and ragged . . . obstructed my view." Burlingame, *A Life:*
vol. 1, 26.

14 "I never went to school . . . I could not understand." Burlingame, *A
Life:* vol. 1, online edition, Tarbell, 43. 130.

14 "Bone and muscle . . . double wasted." Burlingame, *A Life:* vol. 1, 37.

14 "clear proof of Abe's insanity." Burlingame, *A Life:* vol. 1, 29.

14 "I ain't got no education . . . something yet." Burlingame, *A Life:*
vol. 1, 10.

15 "quivered all over . . . ours to us." Wilson and Davis, *Herndon's
Informants,* 40.

15–16 "Abraham Lincoln . . . for fools to read." Library of Congress,
Lincoln as Poet, www.loc.gov/rr/program/bib/prespoetry/al.html.

16 "sink an axe deeper . . . than anyone." Burlingame, *A Life:* vol. 1,
33.

16 "soared above us . . . leadership of the boys." Doris Kearns
Goodwin, *Team of Rivals: The Political Genius of Abraham Lincoln*
(New York, NY: Simon & Schuster, 2005) 49.

17 "go with . . . mitten every time." Burlingame, *A Life:* vol. 1, 42.

17 "I leave it to my audience . . . this one?" Widely attributed to
Lincoln—I have been unable to locate the original source.

2. A Strange and Penniless Boy

18 "It would astonish . . . family distinction." Lincoln, *Collected Works,*
vol. 1, 320.

18 "parental tyranny" Burlingame, *A Life:* vol. 1, 51.

20 "It was the most important . . . less than a day." David Herbert
Donald, *Lincoln* (New York, NY: Simon & Schuster, 1995) 34.

21 "sat down . . . his grief." Goodwin, *Team of Rivals,* 49.

21 "In this sad world . . . what I say." Lincoln to Fanny McCullough,
December 23, 1862, www.abrahamlincolnonline.org/lincoln
/speeches/mccull.htm.

23 "That is a disgrace." Burlingame, *A Life:* vol. 1, 44.

3. Entering Politics

28 "I have no other . . . worthy of their esteem." Lincoln, *Collected
Works,* vol. 1, 5.

30 "I can make a few rabbit tracks" Burlingame, *A Life:* vol. 1, 59.

31 "I felt that . . . soul would be satisfied." William H. Herndon and
Jesse W. Weik, *Abraham Lincoln: The True Story of a Great Life* (New
York, NY: D. Appleton, 1892) 49–50.

33 "No person will deny . . . navigable streams." Lincoln, *Collected
Works,* vol. 1, p. 5.

35 "military hero . . . mosquitoes." Lincoln, *Collected Works,* vol. 1, 510.

35 "I presume . . . all the same." As quoted in the Appendix to the
Congressional Record, proceedings and debates of the 79th Congress

As quoted here: www.nps.gov/liho/learn/historyculture/newsalem. htm, 1st Sess. A2931.

4. A Lawyer

38 "Let reverence . . . courts of justice." Lincoln, *Collected Works*, vol. 1, 112.

41 "more of a hand-shaking campaign than anything else." Burlingame, *A Life:* vol. 1, 82.

41 "See here, Lincoln . . . vote for you." Wilson and Davis, *Herndon's Informants*, 603.

41 "not vote for a man . . . in the crowd." Ward H. Lamon, *The Life of Abraham Lincoln; From his Birth to his Inauguration as President* (Boston, MA: James R. Osgood, 1872) 156. "Make a hand" meant the ability to hold his own in the field.

42 "I voted for Lincoln in opposition to my own creed and faith in politics." Wilson and Davis, *Herndon's Informants*, 450.

43 "reveled in [politics], as a fish does in water, as a bird disports itself on the sustaining air." Burlingame, *A Life:* vol. 1, 88.

44 "I began to read . . . thoroughly absorbed." Tarbell, xiv.

44–45 "declared his love . . . truly." Burlingame, *A Life:* vol. 1, 99–100.

45 "his gloom . . . his mind." George McGovern, *Abraham Lincoln* (New York, NY: Times Books, Henry Holt, 2009) 24.

50–51 Moreover, at any time the Constitution could be amended . . . The Constitution allows for a second method to amend, which has never been successful. Two-thirds of the states can call a national convention, and three-quarters can vote to amend the Constitution.

53 "the institution of slavery . . . the Constitution." Lincoln, *Collected Works*, location 1198.

5. Mary Todd

55 "I have come to the conclusion . . . to have me." Lincoln, *Collected Works*, vol. 1, 119.

57 "That reminds me of a story," Burlingame, *A Life: Volume One*, 268.

59 "could not hold . . . intelligent in the female line." Burlingame, *A Life:* vol. 1, 174.

59–60 "My feet weren't made that way . . . worst way possible." Burlingame, *A Life:* vol. 1, 174–175.

60 "flirted with Douglas . . . said a word." Burlingame, *A Life:* vol. 1, 174.

60 "But I mean . . ." Burlingame, *A Life:* vol. 1, 815. See footnote 366.

60 "impulsive . . . passing emotion." Burlingame, *A Life:* vol. 1, 174.

61 "keep [his] resolves when they are made" Lincoln, *Collected Works*, vol. 1, 289.

62 "I am now the most miserable . . . face on the earth." Lincoln, *Collected Works*, vol. 1, 221.

62 "much alone . . . for months." Justin G. Turner and Linda Levitt Turner, eds., *Mary Todd Lincoln: Her Life and Letters* (New York, NY: Alfred A. Knopf, 1972) 27.

62 "rest from that intensity of thought . . . bitterness of death." Goodwin, *Team of Rivals*, 100.

63 "crazy as a loon" Burlingame, *A Life:* vol. 1, 182.

63 "To hell, I suppose." Herndon and Weik, *The True Story*, 215.

6. A Practical Statesman

64 "A drop of honey . . . sincere friend." From a speech delivered before the Springfield Washington Temperance Society, February 22, 1842, www.abrahamlincolnonline.org/lincoln/speeches/temperance.htm.

65 "pushing him on in his ambition . . . " Burlingame, *A Life:* vol. 1, 211.

65 " . . . nagging her husband on." Wilson and Davis, *Herndon's Informants*, 623.

65 "Now if you should hear . . . very much to go." Lincoln, *Collected Works*, vol. 1, 307.

68 "When I have a particular case . . . fires of the mind." Donald, *Lincoln*, 99.

71 "My childhood's home . . . pleasure in it too." The full poem is available at www.abrahamlincolnonline.org/lincoln/speeches/poetry.htm.

74 "If by your votes . . . evil?" Lincoln, *Collected Works*, vol. 1, 347.

7. Congressman Lincoln

75 "Our government rests . . . change the government." Lincoln, *Collected Works*, vol. 1, 385.

75–76 "Hallooing . . . good Whig, eh?" Burlingame, *A Life*, unedited edition, www.knox.edu/documents/pdfs/LincolnStudies/Burlingame,%20Vol%201,%20Chap%207.pdf.

76 "It is an undeserved honor . . . generous offer." Donald, *Lincoln*, 100.

77 "When you can't find it anywhere else, look in this." Herndon and Weik, *The True Story*, 315.

77 "powerless to withstand their importunities." Herndon and Weik, *The True Story*, 181.

78 "Tirade so fierce . . . get out." Burlingame, *A Life:* vol. 1, 210, fn. 348.

80 "Turn about is fair play." Lincoln made this comment on three separate occasions. Lincoln, *Collected Works*, vol. 1, 350, 352, 359.

81 "most estimable lady" Turner and Turner, *Mary Todd Lincoln*, 87.

81–82 "lay down his knife . . . would follow." Goodwin, *Team of Rivals*, 120.

83 "in the presence of his wife . . . slave prisons." From the Journal of the House of Representatives of the United States, begun December 6, 1847, archive.org/stream/journalofhouseof00unit /journalofhouseof00unit_djvu.txt.

84 "You might have any amount of land . . . you own slaves" Burlingame, vol. 1, p. 461.

84 "highly seductive to thoughtless and giddy headed young men." Wilson and Davis, *Herndon's Informants*, 183.

85 "I hate to stay in this old room . . . forget father." Lincoln, *Collected Works*, vol. 1, 466.

87 "We of the South . . . destroy us as a people." Calhoun, "Positive Good," teachingamericanhistory.org/library/document /slavery-a-positive-good.

89 "is to be President . . . you can see he is not pretty." Burlingame, *A Life:* vol. 1, 211.

89 "My friend . . . rest of your life." Burlingame, *A Life:* vol. 1, 312.

8. Reentering Politics

90 "If a man will stand . . . stop him." Lincoln, *Collected Works*, vol. 2, 283.

90 "Eat, Mary . . . very much." Goodwin, *Team of Rivals,* 131.

91 "My business . . . more painful than pleasant." Lincoln, *Collected Works*, vol. 2, 97.

92 "thunderstruck and stunned; and we reeled and fell in utter confusion." Lincoln, *Collected Works*, vol. 2, 282.

93 "I tell you, Dickey, this nation cannot exist half-slave and half-free." Goodwin, *Team of Rivals,* 133–134.

94 "negro thieves . . . bleeding Kansas." KQED Resource Bank, "Bleeding Kansas," Public Broadcasting Service, www.pbs.org /wgbh/aia/part4/4p2952.html.

96 "Nearly eighty years ago . . . the negro is a human." Lincoln, *Collected Works*, vol. 2, 276–281.

97 "n—worshippers" and "n—agitators" Burlingame, *A Life:* vol. 1, 364.

97 "A man went into a restaurant . . . cheated in some way." Burlingame, *A Life:* vol. 1, 431, paraphrased by the author.

98 "Abraham Lincoln . . . their own way!" Lincoln, *Collected Works*, vol. 2, 230, paraphrased by the author.

99 "If A. can prove . . . superior to your own." Lincoln, *Collected Works*, *A Life:* vol. 2, 222–223.

99 "Make the laboring man . . . white or black." Burlingame, *A Life:* vol. 1, 418.

101 "Do not . . . our forefathers." Burlingame, *A Life:* vol. 1, 157.

102 "warmly encouraged in his aspirations by his wife." Burlingame, *A Life:* vol. 1, 392.

9. *The Birth of the Republican Party*

105 "Repeal the Missouri Compromise . . . will continue to speak." Lincoln, *Collected Works*, vol. 2, 248–249.

108 "the music of an overseer's lash upon a mulatto girl's back . . . souls warmed." Burlingame, *A Life:* vol. 1, 418–420.

108 *Dred Scott v. Sandford*, 60 U.S. 393 (1857). While the Supreme Court's official recording of the name spells Respondent's name as Sandford, in fact, his name was Sanford.

110 "had for more than a century . . . for his benefit." *Dred Scott v. Sandford*.

114 "Isn't it true . . . let it go as it is." Burlingame, *A Life:* vol. 1, 465.

114 "A house divided . . . North as well as South." Lincoln, *Collected Works*, vol. 2, 461.

116 "I will say here . . . inclination to do so." Lincoln, *Collected Works*, vol. 3, 16.

117 "I have no purpose . . . to the contrary." Lincoln, *Collected Works*, vol. 3, 16.

117–118 "I have said that I do not understand . . . let him enjoy." Lincoln, *Collected Works*, vol. 2, 520.

119 "Gloomy as midnight . . . desert me." Burlingame, *A Life:* vol. 1, 550.

119 "Well, Gentlemen . . . wisest thing I ever said." Wilson and Davis, *Herndon's Informants*, 163.

10. President Lincoln

120 "What is conservatism . . . new and untried." Lincoln, *Collected Works*, vol. 3, 537.

120 "Mary insists . . . me as President." Burlingame, *A Life:* vol. 1, 558.

121 "The taste is in my mouth a little." Lincoln, *Collected Works*, vol. 4, 45.

124 "I must go home . . . than I am." Burlingame, *A Life:* vol. 1, 626.

126 "I scarcely know . . . defeat." Turner and Turner, *Mary Todd Lincoln*, 68.

126–127 "Springfield went off like one immense cannon report . . . shouting everywhere." Howard Holzer, "Election Day 1860," *Smithsonian* (November 2008), www.smithsonianmag.com/history /election-day-1860-84266675.

127 "Well, my old friend . . . fault with the jury." Burlingame, *A Life:* vol. 1, 679.

127 Electoral vote: Elections then, as now, were decided through the Electoral College, a complex system of delegates selected by the states: The states elected their delegates to the Electoral College, who then elected the president. Today, while nothing in the Constitution or federal law governs how electoral delegates vote, state laws and political parties generally require them to vote according to the popular vote in their state.

11. A House Divided

129 "A majority held in restraint . . . a free people." Lincoln, *Collected Works*, vol. 4, 261.

133 "We must not be enemies . . . by the better angels of our nature." Lincoln, *Collected Works*, vol. 4, 271.

135 "preserve, protect and defend the Constitution of the United States." The text of the oath of office is given in the Constitution, in Article II, Section 1, Clause 8.

135 "the crowd tossed hats into the air, wiped their eyes, and shouted till they grew hoarse." Burlingame, *A Life:* vol. 1, 61.

136 "when he set his foot down . . . made up his mind." Wilson and Davis, *Herndon's Informants*, 361.

139 "Once let the black man get upon his person the brass letter . . . earned the right to citizenship." National Archives, www.archives .gov/education/lessons/blacks-civil-war.

143 "I cannot imagine that any European power . . . Union for freedom." Burlingame, *A Life:* vol. 2, 333.

143 "it was an exceedingly interesting anecdote, and very apropos, but not altogether a satisfactory answer." Donald, *Lincoln,* 259.

143 "we shall be like the barber . . . cut off his own finger!" Andrew Dickson White, *Old Abe's Jokes* (New York: T. R. Dawley, 1864) 63.

144 "This here talk ain't no use. I never cross a river until I come to it." Burlingame, *A Life:* vol. 2, 334.

144–145 "If I were to try to read . . . would make no difference." Burlingame, *A Life:* vol. 2, 228.

12. The Emancipation Proclamation

147 "I hope to stand firm . . . the country's cause." Lincoln, *Collected Works*, vol. 7, 24.

147 "insurgent forces" Guelzo, *Fateful Lightening*, 161.

148 "Well, Nicolay, my boy is gone—he is actually gone!" Burlingame, *A Life:* vol. 2, 298.

149 "Find out where your enemy is . . . keep moving on." Guelzo, *Fateful Lightening*, 201.

152 "that first step toward that righteousness which exalts a nation." Burlingame, *A Life:* vol. 1, 345.

153 "I have made up my mind . . . carry out my policy." Burlingame, *A Life:* vol. 2, 467.

154 "headquarters in the saddle . . . seems to me this general has his headquarters where his hindquarters ought to be." Appendix to the Cong. Rec., Forty-Seventh Congress, 2nd Sess. (1882), 140.

157 "a genuine representative . . . justice and humanity." Russell Freedman, *Abraham Lincoln and Frederick Douglass: The Story Behind an American Friendship* (Boston, MA: Houghton Mifflin Harcourt, 2012) 69.

159 "shall be then, thenceforward, and forever free." Full text of the Emancipation Proclamation is available at archive.org/stream /theemancipationp22082gut/22082.txt.

159 "We shout for joy . . . his official signature." Goodwin, *Team of Rivals*, 483.

159–160 "the President has as much right . . . doomed to extermination." Burlingame, *A Life:* vol. 2, 416.

160 "with their hands reeking in the blood . . . cross over into our state looking for work/" Burlingame, *A Life:* vol. 2, 420.

162 "When I think of these mere lads . . . longing for home life." Burlingame, *A Life:* vol. 2, 492.

162 "Let him fight instead of being shot." Goodwin, *Team of Rivals*, 539.

165–166 "historic heights . . . our annals" and "tiger is wounded fight to the last." Burlingame, *A Life:* vol. 1, 526–527.

166 "They would kill . . . things to us." Turner and Turner, *Mary Todd Lincoln*, 154.

166 "I seem to be the scapegoat for both North and South" Jean Baker, *Mary Todd Lincoln: A Biography* (New York, NY: W. W. Norton, 1989) 224.

168 "My wife is as handsome . . . I have never fallen out." White House Biographies, "Mary Todd Lincoln," www.whitehouse.gov/1600 /first-ladies/marylincoln.

168 "Four score . . . perish from the earth." Lincoln, *Collected Works*, vol. 7, 18–20.

13. A New Birth of Freedom

170 "As I would not be a slave . . . no democracy." Lincoln, *Collected Works,* vol. 2, 532.

175 "I believe this government was made by white men and for white men." Cong. Globe, 38th Cong. 1st Sess. (1864), 1462.

176 "The President has received yours . . . impartial judge." Lincoln, *Collected Works*, vol. 7, 483.

176 "has gained wisdom . . . beneficial state of things will continue." Burlingame, *A Life:* vol. 2, 689.

177 "alarmed condition . . . profoundest satisfaction" Freedman, *Abraham Lincoln and Frederick Douglass*, 90.

179 "smiled good-naturedly . . . goes the Union, they say." Burlingame, *A Life:* vol. 2, 723.

181 "hook or crook" Burlingame, *A Life:* vol. 2, 748.

181 "As far as I know, there are no peace commissioners in this city, or likely to be in it." Lincoln, *Collected Works*, vol. 8, 248.

184 "Many a poor mother . . . to their mothers." Burlingame, *A Life:* vol. 1, 738.

185 "The sun . . . glory and light." Burlingame, *A Life:* vol. 2, 766.

185 "With malice toward none . . . all nations." Lincoln, *Collected Works*, vol. 8, 333.

186 "Here comes my friend . . . I'm glad you liked it!" Freedman, *Abraham Lincoln and Frederick Douglass*, 100.

189 "It is also unsatisfactory to some . . . the colored man." Lincoln's April 11, 1865, speech, www.gutenberg.org/files/2659/2659 -h/2659-h.htm.

15. Legacy

197 "bore the irons of slavery . . . same dark dungeon." Vorenberg, *Final Freedom: The Civil War, the Abolition of Slavery, adn the Thirteenth Amendment*, 82.

199 "If that word 'male' be inserted, it will take us a century at least to get it out." Alexander Keyssar, *The Right to Vote: The Contested History of Democracy in the United States* (New York, NY: Basic Books, 2000) 143.

203 "always sought the meeting point . . . achieved in practice" Dinesh D'Souza, "Lincoln: Hypocrite or Statesman?" Hoover Institution, Stanford University (April 30, 2005), www.hoover.org/research /lincoln-hypocrite-or-statesman.

Time Line

1809 ✦ **FEBRUARY 12:** Abraham Lincoln is born in a log cabin near what is now Hodgenville, Kentucky.

1811 ✦ The Lincolns move to Knob Creek.

1816 ✦ The Lincolns move to Indiana, settling near what is now Gentryville.

1818 ✦ Lincoln's mother dies of milk sickness.

1819 ✦ Lincoln's father remarries.

1830 ✦ The Lincolns move to Decatur, Illinois.

1831 ✦ Lincoln moves to New Salem, Illinois.

1832 ✦ Lincoln becomes a candidate for the Illinois General Assembly, enlists in the Black Hawk War, and loses the election.

1834 ✦ Lincoln is elected to the Illinois General Assembly. He begins studying law and has a romance with Ann Rutledge.

1835 ✦ Lincoln becomes a leader of the local Whig party.

1836 ✦ **AUGUST 1:** Lincoln is reelected to the General Assembly.

    ✦ **AUGUST 8:** Lincoln earns his law license.

1837 ✦ Moves to Springfield and enters law practice with John Stuart.

1840 ✦ Lincoln and Mary Todd become engaged, then have a falling out.

1842 ✦ **NOVEMBER 4:** Lincoln and Mary Todd get married.

1843 ✦ **AUGUST 1:** The Lincolns' first son, Robert Todd, is born.

1844 ✦ Lincoln campaigns for Henry Clay and returns for the first time to his boyhood home in Indiana.

1844 ✦ Lincoln and Herndon become law partners.

1846 ✦ The Lincolns' second son, Edward Baker, is born. Lincoln is nominated as the Whig candidate to Congress.

1847–1849 ✦ Lincoln served as a congressman, representing the Seventh Congressional District in Illinois.

1849 ✦ Giving up on politics, Lincoln returns to Springfield to practice law.

1850 ✦ FEBRUARY 1: Edward dies.

✦ DECEMBER 21: A third son, William Wallace, is born in December.

1854 ✦ After a long break from politics, Lincoln reenters politics to oppose the Kansas-Nebraska Act.

1855 ✦ Lincoln runs for the Senate but is not chosen by the Illinois legislature.

1858 ✦ Lincoln is nominated to be the Republican candidate for the Senate but loses to Democrat Stephen Douglas.

1860 ✦ MAY 18: Lincoln is nominated to be the Republican candidate for president.

✦ NOVEMBER 6: Lincoln is elected president of the United States.

1861 ✦ MARCH 4: Lincoln is inaugurated.

✦ APRIL 12: The Civil War begins when Confederate artillery open fire on Fort Sumter.

✦ JULY 21: The Union army suffers a defeat at Bull Run in Virginia.

1862 ✦ **FEBRUARY 2-12:** Union general Grant captures Fort Henry and Fort Donelson in Tennessee.

✦ **FEBRUARY 20:** William Wallace Lincoln dies.

✦ **APRIL 6-7:** Confederates get the better of General Grant in the Battle of Shiloh in Tennessee. The battle saw more casualties than all the previous American wars combined.

✦ **APRIL 16:** Lincoln signs an act abolishing slavery in Washington, D.C.

✦ **JUNE 25-JULY 1:** Union general McClellan retreats after the Seven Days' Battles near Richmond. Both armies suffer heavy losses.

✦ **SEPTEMBER 17:** Confederates retreat to Virginia after encountering superior Union forces at Antietam in Maryland.

✦ **SEPTEMBER 22:** Lincoln issues the preliminary Emancipation Proclamation.

1863 ✦ **JANUARY 1:** Lincoln issues the final Emancipation Proclamation and moves to enlist blacks in the Union army.

✦ **APRIL 30-MAY 6:** Union forces suffer defeat at the Battle of Chancellorsville in Virginia.

✦ **JULY 1-3:** The war turns in the favor of the Union after the Union victory at Gettysburg.

✦ **JULY 4:** Grant defeats the Confederates at Vicksburg, putting the Union in control of the entire Mississippi River.

✦ **NOVEMBER 19:** Lincoln delivers the Gettysburg Address.

Time Line

1864 ✶ **MARCH 9**: Lincoln appoints General Grant to command all of the Union armies.

✶ **APRIL 8**: The Senate passes the Thirteenth Amendment.

✶ **SEPTEMBER 1**: Sherman's army captures Atlanta. Lincoln approves Sherman's March to the Sea.

✶ **NOVEMBER 8**: Lincoln is reelected, defeating McClellan, winning 55 percent of the popular vote.

1865 ✶ **JANUARY 31**: The House passes the Thirteenth Amendment and it is sent to the states for ratification.

✶ **MARCH 4**: Lincoln is re-inaugurated.

✶ **APRIL 9**: Lee surrenders to Grant following the Battle of Appomattox Court House in Virginia.

✶ **APRIL 11**: Lincoln gives his last speech.

✶ **APRIL 14**: Lincoln is assassinated.

✶ **DECEMBER 9**: When Georgia ratifies the Thirteenth Amendment, slavery ceases to exist in the United States.

Selected Writings of Abraham Lincoln

Part I of "My Childhood Home I See Again"

My childhood home I see again,
And sadden with the view;
And still, as memory crowds my brain,
There's pleasure in it too.

O Memory! thou midway world
'Twixt earth and paradise,
Where things decayed and loved ones lost
In dreamy shadows rise,

And, freed from all that's earthly vile,
Seem hallowed, pure, and bright,
Like scenes in some enchanted isle
All bathed in liquid light.

As dusky mountains please the eye
When twilight chases day;
As bugle-notes that, passing by,
In distance die away;

As leaving some grand waterfall,
We, lingering, list its roar–

So memory will hallow all
We've known, but know no more.

Near twenty years have passed away
Since here I bid farewell
To woods and fields, and scenes of play,
And playmates loved so well.

Where many were, but few remain
Of old familiar things;
But seeing them, to mind again
The lost and absent brings.

The friends I left that parting day,
How changed, as time has sped!
Young childhood grown, strong manhood gray,
And half of all are dead.

I hear the loved survivors tell
How nought from death could save,
Till every sound appears a knell,
And every spot a grave.

I range the fields with pensive tread,
And pace the hollow rooms,
And feel (companion of the dead)
I'm living in the tombs.

THE GETTYSBURG ADDRESS

Delivered by Lincoln during the American Civil War at the dedication of the Soldier's National Cemetary in Gettysburg, Pennsylvania, November 19, 1863

Four score and seven years ago our fathers brought forth on this continent, a new nation, conceived in Liberty, and dedicated to the proposition that all men are created equal.

Now we are engaged in a great civil war, testing whether that nation, or any nation so conceived and so dedicated, can long endure. We are met on a great battle-field of that war. We have come to dedicate a portion of that field, as a final resting place for those who here gave their lives that that nation might live. It is altogether fitting and proper that we should do this.

But, in a larger sense, we can not dedicate–we can not consecrate–we can not hallow–this ground. The brave men, living and dead, who struggled here, have consecrated it, far above our poor power to add or detract. The world will little note, nor long remember what we say here, but it can never forget what they did here. It is for us the living, rather, to be dedicated here to the unfinished work which they who fought here have thus far so nobly advanced. It is rather for us to be here dedicated to the great task remaining before us—that from these honored dead we take increased devotion to that cause for which they gave the last full measure of devotion—that we here highly resolve that these dead shall not have died in vain—that this nation, under God, shall have a new birth of freedom—and that government of the people, by the people, for the people, shall not perish from the earth.

CORRESPONDENCE WITH ELEVEN-YEAR-OLD GRACE BEDELL

SHOWING WHEN—AND PERHAPS WHY— LINCOLN GREW A BEARD

N Y
Westfield Chataugue Co
Oct 15. 1860
Hon A B Lincoln

Dear Sir

My father has just home from the fair and brought home
your picture and Mr. Hamlin's. I am a little girl only eleven
years old, but want you should be President of the United
States very much so I hope you wont think me very bold to
write to such a great man as you are. Have you any little girls
about as large as I am if so give them my love and tell her
to write to me if you cannot answer this letter. I have got 4
brother's and part of them will vote for you any way and if
you will let your whiskers grow I will try and get the rest of
them to vote for you you would look a great deal better for
your face is so thin. All the ladies like whiskers and they would
tease their husband's to vote for you and then you would be
President. My father is a going to vote for you and if I was a
man I would vote for you to but I will try and get every one

to vote for you that I can I think that rail fence around your picture makes it look very pretty I have got a little baby sister she is nine weeks old and is just as cunning as can be. When you direct your letter dirffiefflct to Grace Bedell Westfield Chatauque County New York

I must not write any more answer this letter right off

Good bye
Grace Bedell

October 19, 1860
Springfield, Illinois
Miss. Grace Bedell

My dear little Miss.

Your very agreeable letter of the 15th. is received.

I regret the necessity of saying I have no daughters. I have three sons—one seventeen, one nine, and one seven, years of age. They, with their mother, constitute my whole family.

As to the whiskers, having never worn any, do you not think people would call it a piece of silly affection if I were to begin it now? Your very sincere well-wisher

A. Lincoln

Afterward, Lincoln grew a beard, which he wore the rest of his life.

Bibliography

Primary Sources

Lincoln's speeches and letters are available at www.abrahamlincolnonline
.org/index.html.

Congressional Record, memory.loc.gov/ammem/amlaw/lwcg.html.

Library of Congress, *Lincoln as Poet.* www.loc.gov/rr/program/bib
/prespoetry/al.html.

Lincoln, Abraham, *The Collected Works of Abraham Lincoln.* Springfield,
IL: The Abraham Lincoln Association, quod.lib.umich.edu/l
/lincoln/ and www.gutenberg.org/files/3253/3253-h/3253-h.htm.

National Archives, www.archives.gov/education/lessons/
blacks-civil-war.

University of Illinois University Online Digital Collection of Primary
Source Materials at lincoln.lib.niu.edu.

White House Biographies, "Mary Todd Lincoln," www.whitehouse
.gov/1600/first-ladies/marylincoln.

Books

Baker, Jean. *Mary Todd Lincoln: A Biography.* New York, NY: W.W.
Norton, 1989.

Burlingame, Michael. *Abraham Lincoln: A Life,* 2 vols. Baltimore, MD:
Johns Hopkins University Press, 2012. Reprint edition, Kindle
edition.

———. *Abraham Lincoln: A Life,* unedited edition. John Hopkins
University Press, Knox College, and the author have made available
the entire unedited four thousand page, exhaustively researched

manuscript at www.knox.edu/about-knox/lincoln-studies-center /burlingame-abraham-lincoln-a-life.

Chapman, John Jay. *William Lloyd Garrison*. Boston, MA: Atlantic Monthly Press, 1913. archive.org/details/williamlloydgarr02chap.

Cox, LaWanda. *Lincoln and Black Freedom: A Study in Presidential Leadership*. Columbia, SC: University of South Carolina Press, 1981, 1994.

Donald, David Herbert. *Lincoln*. New York, NY: Simon & Schuster, 1995.

Freedman, Russell. *Abraham Lincoln and Frederick Douglass: The Story Behind an American Friendship*. Boston, MA: Houghton Mifflin Harcourt, 2012.

Goodwin, Doris Kearns. *Team of Rivals: The Political Genius of Abraham Lincoln*. New York, NY: Simon & Schuster, 2005.

Guelzo, Allen C. *Fateful Lightning*. New York, NY: Oxford University Press, 2012.

Herndon, William H. and Weik, Jesse W. *Abraham Lincoln: The True Story of a Great Life*. New York, NY: D. Appleton, 1892. archive.org/ details/abrahamlincolntr01hern.

Keyssar, Alexander. *The Right to Vote: The Contested History of Democracy in the United States*. New York, NY: Basic Books, 2000.

Lamon, Ward H. *The Life of Abraham Lincoln; From his Birth to his Inauguration as President*. Boston, MA: James R. Osgood and Company, 1872. archive.org/details/lifeofabrahamlin00lamouoft.

Lincoln, Abraham. *Collected Writings of Abraham Lincoln*, 7 vols. Waxkeep, 2013. Kindle edition.

McGovern, George. *Abraham Lincoln*. New York, NY: Times Books, Henry Holt, 2009.

Tarbell, Ida M. *The Life of Abraham Lincoln: Drawn from original sources and containing many speeches, letters and telegrams hitherto unpublished*. New York, NY: New York History Society, 1924. archive. org/details/lifeofabrahamlin03iltarb.

——————. *Selections from the Letters, Speeches, and State Papers of Abraham Lincoln*. New York, NY: Ginn, 1911. archive.org/details/ selectionsfrom2849linc.

Turner, Justin G. and Turner, Linda Levitt, eds. *Mary Todd Lincoln: Her Life and Letters*. New York, NY: Alfred A. Knopf, 1972. archive.org /details/marytoddlincolnh00just.

Vorenberg, Michael, *Final Freedom: The Civil War, the Abolition of Slavery, and the Thirteenth Amendment*. New York, NY: Cambridge University Press: 2001.

White, Andrew Dickson. *Old Abe's Jokes*. New York, NY: T. R. Dawley, 1864.

Wilson, Douglas L. and Davis, Rodney O., eds. *Herndon's Informants: Letters, Interviews, and Statements about Abraham Lincoln*. Chicago, IL: University of Illinois Press, 1998.

Articles

D'Souza, Dinesh, "Lincoln: Hypocrite or Statesman?" Published by the Hoover Institution, Stanford University, April 30, 2005. www.hoover.org/research/lincoln-hypocrite-or-statesman.

Holzer, Howard, "Election Day 1860," *Smithsonian*, November 2008. www.smithsonianmag.com/history/election-day-1860-84266675.

KQED Resource Bank, "Bleeding Kansas," Public Broadcasting Service. www.pbs.org/wgbh/aia/part4/4p2952.html.

White House website biographies: "Mary Todd Lincoln." whitehouse.gov/1600/first-ladies/marylincoln.

Acknowledgments

I owe a special thanks to Ari Kelman, professor of history at the University of California–Davis and expert in the Civil War era, who read the manuscript for accuracy and provided many insightful comments. Any remaining errors, of course, are my own. Thanks also to the heroes of historical preservation who have made available to the public volumnous original sources, including the National Archives Online Records, the Abraham Lincoln Association, the Library of Congress, Project Gutenberg, and the University of Illinois Online Digital Collection.

Thank you to all members of the talented and dedicated Abrams team. Thanks in particular to Howard Reeves, editor beyond compare, designer Sara Corbett (who once again turned a mere manuscript into a work of art), and Tom McNellis and Sonya Maynard, two sharp-eyed and meticulous readers who made sure every *i* is properly dotted and every *t* properly crossed. Thanks also to Emily Daluga, who was always there to offer help and encouragement.

Last but definitely not least, thanks to my first readers: Betsy Wattenberg, Carole Greeley, and Andy Schloss.

Index

Note: Page numbers in *italics* refer to illustrations.

Index